BERLITZ®

EGYPT

D1501431

 By the staff of Berlitz Guides

16th edition (1992/1993)

Updated or revised 1992, 1991, 1990, 1988, 1986, 1985, 1984,
1983, 1982

How to use our guide

- All the practical information, hints and tips that you will need before and during the trip start on page 102.
- For general background, see the sections Egypt and the Egyptians, p. 6, and A Brief History, p. 12.
- All the sights to see are listed between pages 24 and 83. Our own choice of sights most highly recommended is pinpointed by the Berlitz traveller symbol.
- Entertainment, nightlife and all other leisure activities are described between pages 84 and 95, while information on restaurants and cuisine is to be found on pages 95 to 101.
- Finally, there is an index at the back of the book, pp. 126–128.

Found an error or an omission in this Berlitz Guide? Or a change or new feature we should know about? Our editor would be happy to hear from you, and a postcard would do. Be sure to include your name and address, since in appreciation for a useful suggestion, we'd like to send you a travel guide. Write to: Berlitz Publishing Co. Ltd., London Road, Wheatley, Oxford OX9 1YR, England.

Although we make every effort to ensure the accuracy of all the information in this book, changes occur incessantly. We cannot therefore take responsibility for facts, prices, addresses and circumstances in general that are constantly subject to alteration.

Text: Tom Brosnahan
Photography: Luc Chessex; p. 94 Bernard Joliat
Layout: Doris Haldemann
Illustrations: Aude Aquoise
We are grateful to Egypt-Air and Assem Tawfik as well as Mounira Fouad and Abdel Rahman of the Egyptian Tourist Office in Geneva for their valuable assistance. We would also like to thank Susan Brooks Gaynor, Jocelyn Gohary and Jeanne McAlister for their help in updating this guide.
4 Cartography: Falk Falk-Verlag, Hamburg.

Contents

Cover picture: Pyramids and Sphinx of Giza
Photo pp. 2–3: Tomb painting at Valley of the Kings

Egypt and the Egyptians

Vast expanses of burning Saharan wasteland, the limitless sands broken only by dusty caravan tracks: how could such terrain have given birth 5,000 years ago to one of man's most awe-inspiring civilizations? Almost every Egyptian mystery has the same solution: the Nile. Gathering waters from deep in Africa, the mighty river makes its way through the desert to the Mediterranean Sea. Without the Nile, there would be no Egypt.

To understand the impor-

tance of the river for Egyptians, stand on its western bank at Aswan. Here, the desert reaches so close to the water that you can pick up a handful of sand and throw it in. For more than 600 miles—from Abu Simbel to Cairo—narrow fields full of irrigated crops line the banks. The cloudless sky adds its blessing, the hot sun nurturing no fewer than two harvests a year. The early Egyptians saw divinity in the sun which returned faithfully every day: they

Egyptian extremes: slow caravans in vast deserts, and fast-moving Cairo buses always packed full.

named it Ra, and raised great temples in its honour.

What happened to these ancient Egyptians? Believe it or not, their descendants still live along the Nile. They accepted Christianity as taught them by Saint Mark, and founded one of Christendom's oldest churches. Called Copts, they still play a significant role in their country's affairs, and Coptic churches can be found in almost all Egyptian towns.

Between 1100 and 332 B.C. came Libyans, Persians and black Africans from Nubia. Then, around the 7th century, Arabs started to pour into Egypt's rich delta, adding their own languages and customs which still thrive today.

Egypt has always held an irresistible fascination for tourists and it's not difficult to understand why. Pyramids, palms, the Nile, the desert, the Sphinx—all these are enough to make any traveller dream of at least one trip to Egypt in a lifetime. But scratch the surface of a pyramid and you'll find Egypt's true glory, for this is a land whose history and ancient civilization are of inestimable value to archaeologists and anthropologists, theologians and philosophers, art historians and other scholars from almost every field of culture and learning.

And it is this deeply rooted sense of history, which you can sense even today, that makes the country unique. As you visit the four mighty stone figures at the Ramesis II monument in Abu Simbel, it's impossible not to feel a certain awe about a civilization which gave a pharaoh the status of a god. Walking through the sacred temples of Luxor and Karnak and the eerie city of the dead at Thebes will make you realize how serious these ancient Egyptians were about their religion. Elsewhere, you'll constantly see the sights and hear the names that make up the colourful mosaic of Egyptian life: Memphis, Horus, Tutankhamon, Antony and Cleopatra, El-Alamein, Alexandria, the Suez Canal. But just as the Rosetta Stone provided the clue to ancient hieroglyphs, the key to the heart of modern Egypt is, undeniably, Cairo.

Compared to the eternal life of the river, Cairo is a "new" city—only 1,000 years old. In the shadow of Giza's pyramids, Cairenes have raised countless monuments to the glory of Islam and made their city the cultural capital of Arabic civiliza-

Ramesis II repeats himself at awe-inspiring Abu Simbel temple.

tion. Throughout the world, Moslems still look to Cairo as the treasure-house of Islamic art, architecture and learning.

As capital of the most populous Arab nation on earth, Cairo confronts urgent problems. Its population grows at the incredible rate of nearly 4,000 persons a day; even crumbling medieval tombs have been converted to dwellings in an effort to house them all. The city's streets are thronged with armies of pedestrians and legions of cars, all stirring up the blanket

Cruising down the Nile—felucca sailors certainly know the ropes.

of fine desert dust which infrequent and brief rains can never wash away. Noise is a constant bother. Public services are so overtaxed that buses run with passengers on the fenders and hanging out of the windows.

With all its excess population, Cairo is not the land of do-it-yourself, but of have-someone-do-it-for-you. From carrying your luggage to fetching a newspaper, you'll get more help than you need for a small tip.

But despite difficult problems, Egyptians are eternally hopeful. Every day the newspapers announce another momentous new project designed to catapult the country into the future. The plans may well get bogged down in skeins of red tape, but one can't give up hope. After all, the Aswan High Dam performed modern miracles, controlling the annual flooding of the Nile which had occurred since the beginning of time, and providing much-needed electricity for the country's requirements. In any case, it doesn't help to worry.

Long-suffering Cairenes draw confidence from their city's triumphant past and their country's glorious history: Egypt is eternal, the Nile's not going to stop flowing. As for the inconveniences of city life, *ma'alish!* Never mind!

A Brief History

Years, even centuries, lose meaning as one leaps back in time to the misty ages of 3000 B.C.* Before this date, Egyptian life is shrouded in mystery, though we know that the inhabitants were an artistically gifted and vigorous people. They already had a sophisticated hieroglyphic symbol system, and when they invented papyrus by pounding strips of Nile reeds together the written history of ancient Egypt began to unfold.

Old and Middle Kingdoms

King Menes (1st Dynasty, 3000 B.C.) united Upper and Lower Egypt, and was the first to wear the "double crown" so often seen in pharaonic art. The capital was at Memphis, a short distance south of Cairo. Unity brought Egypt wealth, power and progress, and some three centuries later the Old Kingdom (2780–2250 B.C.) headed by King Zoser of the 3rd Dynasty was established. He built the step pyramid of Saqqara, inaugurating the era of the great pyramids. Within 200 years mathematics and man-

power organization had advanced so far that Cheops and his son Chephren were able to construct the colossal pyramids and sphinx at Giza. Crowning this astounding human achievement with the halo of divinity, pharaohs of the 5th Dynasty (2440–2315 B.C.) proclaimed themselves to be sons of the great sun god Ra. But saying one is a god and being a god are different matters, and as time wore on royal authority declined. The Old Kingdom

---

* All dates given before the birth of Christ must be regarded as approximate.

was brought to an end by civil war around 2250 B.C.

The Middle Kingdom lasted over four centuries (2000–1570 B.C.) during which time Egypt re-established itself as a rich and strong nation. Pharaohs stood at the top of a feudal order, and powerful nobles controlled each of the *nomes* (provinces) of the kingdom. Supported by his vassals, the king marched at the head of his army from the new capital at Thebes (Luxor) south to Nubia and east

King Zoser's Step Pyramid set off the pyramid-building craze.

into Palestine, conquering all in his path. Foreign adventures could be afforded because of the immense new wealth brought by significant advances in irrigation, especially in the desert province of Fayyoum.

As the conquerors' fortunes increased, their lands became more and more desirable to Egypt's warlike neighbours. **13**

One enemy people, the Hyksos, had a secret weapon to overcome even the bravest and most determined Egyptian foot-soldier: the horse chariot. When in the 17th century B.C. they rolled swiftly across Sinai and into the fertile delta, the pharaohs were forced to retreat to Thebes (Luxor). Triumphantly the Hyksos chiselled signs of their victories on the walls of tombs and temples, where figures of horses and

Historical Key

Egyptian history is so long it soon becomes bewildering. (By the time you've mastered it all, you'll be ready for a Ph.D.) Here's a simplified key to the major periods:

Old Kingdom	3000–2250 B.C.	1st to 6th Dynasties; pyramids at Giza and Saqqara
Middle Kingdom	2000–1570 B.C.	11th and 12th Dynasties; Hyksos chariot invasion
New Kingdom	1570–1100 B.C.	18th to 20th Dynasties; tombs and temples at Luxor, Abu Simbel
Libyan, Nubian, Assyrian, Persian, Greek Invasions	1100–332 B.C.	21st to 30th Dynasties; decline and civil strife
Ptolemaic Period	332–30 B.C.	Ptolemies I to XIV; Alexander the Great's successors
Roman-Byzantine Period	30 B.C.–A.D. 639	Saint Mark brings Christianity about A.D. 40
Arab Empire	639–1251	Umayyad, Abbasid, Fatimid, Ayyubid Dynasties
Mameluke Dynasties	1251–1517	Cairo mosques and mausoleums
Ottoman Turkish Period	1517–1914	Mohammed Ali gains control, 1811; Suez Canal opens, 1869
Kingdom of Egypt	1914–1952	Mohammed Ali Dynasty; British control
Republican Period	Begins 1953	Aswan High Dam completed, 1972

wheeled vehicles remain to this day. For a century the Hyksos ruled Lower Egypt, but their unassailable power stopped where the chariots could go no farther, at the southern tip of the flat and easily crossed delta.

New Kingdom

The threat from the Hyksos had forced the pharaohs to think over the way the country was run, and after their expulsion in 1570 B.C. a number of reforms were undertaken. First, the rulers succeeded in taking away the power of the great feudal nobles and concentrating it all in their own hands. Then they built chariots, thus improving their military capacity, and soon Egypt became an imperial state, well-organized, disciplined and headed by a monarch greedy for foreign conquests and personal glory. During the New Kingdom (1570–1100 B.C.) ancient Egypt reached the pinnacle of its splendour. The massive temples and tombs at Luxor, Karnak and Abu Simbel were built, and Egyptian armies brought back rich booty and hundreds of slaves from Syria and deep in Africa. The wealth of the country was unparalleled, and much of it went to glorify the god-kings who ruled it.

Some of Egypt's greatest rulers were those of the 18th Dynasty. The three pharaohs named Thutmose vastly extended the empire's borders. Hatshepsut, wife of Thutmose II and stepmother of Thutmose III, ruled for a time as queen of Egypt, and built herself a fabulous funerary temple at Deir el-Bahari. Amenophis III (1417–1379 B.C.) reigned when New Kingdom Egypt was at its glittering zenith. He made large contributions to the building of the Great Temple of Amon at Karnak as well as two gigantic seated figures called the Colossi of Memnon, fashioned in his own image. His son Amenophis IV ignored statecraft and warfare to concentrate on mystical matters, and decreed a new religion: the age-old pantheon of Egyptian gods was to be displaced by the One True God, Aton, whose symbol was a simple solar disc with beneficent rays extending to earth. Amenophis changed his own name to Akhenaton ("He Who Pleases Aton"), and with Queen Nefertiti moved his capital to the place now called Tell El-Amarna in Middle Egypt. But he made bitter enemies of the powerful priests of Amon at Thebes. When he died, the country was in disarray and his young son-in-law Tutankhaton **15**

(1361–1351 B.C.—who later changed his name to Tutankhamon) had such a short reign that it was impossible to restore order.

The 18th Dynasty ended as power was usurped by an energetic and able soldier, Ramesis I, founder of the 19th Dynasty. His successor, Seti, won back all of Egypt's foreign possessions by renewed conquests. Then came Ramesis II. This pharaoh had some trouble maintaining the empire, but none in becoming the greatest and most prolific builder Egypt had ever known. His long reign (1304–1237 B.C.) saw the huge temple rise at Abu Simbel, and the great hypostyle hall finished at Karnak, plus countless other gigantic monuments, usually containing a generous ration of statues in his own image. With a firm hand Ramesis II subdued the Semitic tribes which had been a cause of disorder in his eastern provinces. One tribe, the Israelites, he kept under strict control for years before allowing them to leave captivity in Egypt and return to the land of their forefathers.

Pharaohs of the 20th Dynasty preserved Egypt's greatness until 1100 B.C. After that, although later dynasties struggled to return to past glory, none could regain it. Foreign invasions became frequent, and by 332 B.C. the last Egyptian pharaoh had fallen from the throne forever. Alexander the Great conquered the country with little resistance, and pharaonic Egypt's fabled life was at an end.

Under Greece and Rome

When Alexander died and the Hellenistic empire fell in 323 B.C., his generals seized control of the fragments. The governor of Egypt, Ptolemy, assumed the title of pharaoh in 305 but the country was divided into two cultures now, and the Hellenistic dominated the Egyptian. Alexandria, the conqueror's city on the Mediterranean shore, was the most civilized and important in the Hellenistic world. But the power of learning and the excellent library which were Alexandria's glory could do little against the legions of Rome.

For twenty years (51–30 B.C.) Queen Cleopatra VII used wit and charm—first on Caesar, then on the Roman general Mark Antony—to keep her country free (see box). But Caesar's heir, Octavius (later Augustus), was immune to her fascination and set out to take control of Egypt. When Mark Antony was defeated at the naval battle of Actium (30 B.C.) the queen committed suicide,

Cleopatra

Lots of Ptolemaic princesses were given the name Cleopatra, but it was Cleopatra VII (69–30 B.C.) who left her mark on history. Married to her younger brother Ptolemy XII when she was seventeen years old, she later overthrew him with Caesar's aid. She followed the conqueror to Rome, deserted her second husband—another brother—and eventually bore a son, whom she named Caesarion. (It has never been unquestionably established that Caesarion's true father was Julius Caesar, but it suited everybody to believe it at the time.) For a while Caesarion co-reigned with his mother as Ptolemy XIV.

Some time after Caesar's murder, Marc Antony showed up in Egypt and also fell quickly and completely under Cleopatra's bewitching spell. They were married in 36 B.C. At the end of her reign, after the crushing naval defeat at Actium, she had a servant bring her a basket of figs, containing a serpent. She bit a fig and the snake bit her.

Despite the evident charms she seems to have had for Julius Caesar and Mark Antony, historians record that Cleopatra was neither strikingly beautiful nor popular with the Romans, who either feared or despised her.

and Hellenistic Egypt died with her. For centuries to come the land would be only a distant province of the Roman Empire, ruled first from Rome and later from Constantinople.

The Arab Empire

The wave of conquering armies which poured forth from Arabia in the 7th century is one of the most baffling phenomena in history. Before the Prophet Mohammed's time, the Arabs consisted of only a few dozen Semitic tribes living in a hot and dusty land. To earn their dates and camel's milk, they traded by camel caravan or carried out raids on their neighbours. But with the coming of Islam ("Submission to God's Will"), the Arabs set out on conquests which were to change the world.

Mohammed, a merchant in the city of Mecca, was a pensive man who would go off to a cool cave in the mountains to think and ponder. During one such retreat in A.D. 612 he heard a celestial voice commanding him to write and communicate his vision. During the next twenty years, until his death in 632, Mohammed produced the 114 *suras* (verses) which make up the Koran, the beautiful work which became the poetry, law and inspiration of the Moslem world. **17**

In the early years of Islam, believers were organized into a small, close-knit society headed by Mohammed himself. As the community expanded, armies were formed, and military operations begun. Within a century of Mohammed's death, Arab forces had conquered all the Middle East including Persia, all of North Africa, and even parts of Spain and France.

Egypt was among the first countries to fall, invaded by the Arabs in 639. They made their military camp, El-Fustat, the country's capital. Within 300 years Egypt had become one of the Arab Empire's most important political, military and religious centres. Then, in about 968, a powerful dynasty called the Fatimids swept in from the Maghreb to seize Egypt and establish a new capital, Misr Al-Qahira, the City of Mars. Despite the decadence that was later to set in, Fatimid rule was vigorous at first and Cairo enjoyed one of its richest cultural periods during the two centuries of domination. The renowned mosque and university of El-Azhar date from these times and still remain a spiritual beacon to all Islam, the buildings recalling the highest glory of Fatimid architecture.

18 The empire of the Fatimids

was overrun by the armies of Saladin in 1169. Saladin, famous for his campaigns against the Crusaders in Palestine and Syria, established his own dynasty in Egypt, the Ayyubids. His descendants were ousted by a new wave of usurpers, mostly Turkish soldiers who had been slaves *(mameluke)* of the Ayyubids. In a series of short and violent reigns, Mameluke strongmen succeeded one another from 1251 to 1517. Despite the instability of their rule, Mameluke might spread through Syria and Palestine. In Cairo, they built countless palaces and mosques of exquisite beauty.

Mameluke power was defeated, but not destroyed, when Egypt was conquered by the fast-moving and efficient armies of the Ottoman Turks in 1517. Three years later, Suleiman the Magnificent came to the throne in Constantinople (Istanbul), ushering in the Ottoman Empire's most brilliant and powerful era. But it didn't last long and when he died his dominions began a period of decline lasting some three and a half centuries. The Egyptian province lost the benefits of

El-Azhar, glory of Islamic Cairo, is the Oxford of the Moslem world.

efficient government and internal order as provincial Mameluke lords clamoured for many of their old prerogatives from the Ottoman pasha in Cairo. Instability returned with the Mameluke rulers and Egypt lived from crisis to crisis in a decadent and backward culture.

Napoleon and Mohammed Ali
The modern world first came into contact with Egypt when a French military expedition headed by a young officer named Napoleon Bonaparte reached Alexandria in 1798. Though their primary interest was to block Britain's Red Sea route to India, the expedition included a group of scientists and archaeologists. Napoleon's efforts brought a certain order and discipline to Egypt's government for a short time, and laid the foundation for later archaeological expeditions. In the momentous Battle of Abukir (1798), the British destroyed the French fleet. Three years later the remnants of the French force returned home. Egypt seemed ready to slip into torpor and anarchy again.

France's Empress Eugenie, Austria's Franz-Josef, Egypt's Ismail in glittering array as Suez opens.

Among the Ottoman troops who had arrived to counter the French invasion was a young officer called Mohammed Ali. With considerable cunning and force, he succeeded in seizing power and having himself appointed Pasha of Egypt by the sultan. Then on May 1, 1811, he invited all his rivals, the Mameluke notables, to a banquet in the Citadel at Cairo. As each Mameluke entered the thick stone walls, the gates were slammed shut behind him and the new pasha's troops quietly removed his head from his body. Mameluke political power, an important factor in Egypt since 1251, ended for good that night.

Fascinated by glimpses of modern methods he had seen in Napoleon's army, Mohammed Ali proceeded to reform his own and to build a fleet on Western lines, using European advisors. Moves were made to modernize agriculture and commerce, and cotton was planted in newly irrigated lands. The country started to produce great wealth, and though the people remained desperately poor, the ruler was fabulously rich and powerful. Between 1832 and 1841 Mohammed Ali waged war on his sovereign in Istanbul twice and almost succeeded in capturing the Ottoman capital. Forced to recognize the virtually independent power of his onetime vassal, the sultan decreed that the office of Pasha of Egypt should be hereditary in the house of Mohammed Ali. Later this title of *pasha* was upgraded to *khedive*, just short of "king".

But later rulers of the House of Mohammed Ali could not live up to their ancestor's energy and vision. Khedive Ismail, who ruled from 1863 to 1879, championed the plan for a Suez Canal, but his ambitious undertakings were financed by unscrupulous bankers. When the khedive could not repay the millions in gold which had been lent him at usurious rates of interest, he was forced by the European powers to accept British and French financial "advisors" in his government. The British soon succeeded in gaining political and military control of the country as well.

The 20th Century

During the First World War, Egypt's strategic position was crucial to the British, and Cairo was the staging-point for the Allied offensive which wrested Palestine, Arabia and Syria from Ottoman control. Even before the Ottoman Empire fell, Egypt's British governors had declared the puppet khedive's independence from his Turkish sovereign. Prince Fuad styled himself King of Egypt when he came to the throne in 1917, but real power was still in the hands of foreigners.

After the war, nationalist sentiments crystallized in the Wafd Party, led by Saad Zaghloul Pasha. When free elections for a Chamber of Deputies were held in 1924, the anti-British Wafd won a large majority of seats. It continued to be the prime nationalist force for decades afterwards.

The Second World War brought renewed military importance to Egypt. In 1940 an Italian invasion force from Libya pushed deep into Egypt before being turned back by British Empire troops. In the following year General Rommel and an army of trained desert fighters recaptured the ground and rolled swiftly into Egypt. They were stopped at El Alamein, only 60 miles from Alexandria, in 1942. By the end of the year the tide of war had turned in favour of the Allies, and Egypt was again securely in British hands.

King Farouk had come to the Egyptian throne in 1936, a handsome and promising youth trained in a British officers' school. Despite his good intentions, Farouk soon succumbed to the oriental atmosphere of palace intrigue and luxurious living. Government suffered, and military defeat in Palestine (1948) was followed by diplomatic defeat when the king tried to claim full control over the Sudan and the Suez Canal. Unrest grew, until he was overthrown in 1952. A group of military officers led by General Mohammed Naguib took over. After a short time, Naguib was replaced by the real mastermind of the revolution, Colonel Gamal Abdel Nasser.

The country was declared a republic on 18th June, 1953, and Nasser remained in power for 17 years. Despite his authoritarian rule, it was during this period that Egypt regained a sense of national identity: under an Egyptian-run government the country rapidly emerged as a leader of the Third World nations and started to overhaul and modernize the economy. The symbol for this effort became the Aswan High Dam, whose giant power stations generate huge quantities of electricity supplying a third of the country's needs.

When President Sadat succeeded Nasser in 1970, his more moderate influence provided the counter-balance the country so desperately needed.

Immense power of the Nile churns out millions of kilowatts (Aswan).

Egypt's energy and resources had been continually under strain as a result of the recurrent wars with Israel. In 1948, 1956, 1967 and 1973 hostilities had broken out between the two countries. It was under Sadat that the historic peace treaty between Egypt and Israel was finally signed in the U.S. in 1979; fiercely opposed by other Arab leaders, it was one reason for Sadat's assassination in 1981.

From ancient pharaohs to modern statesmen, from kings and queens, generals and rulers of every description Egypt's destiny has been formed and handed down from generation to generation through the ages.

Egypt's moderate political stance over the last years—in spite of its internal problems—has won it international respect, from which tourism has greatly benenfitted.

23

Where to Go

Cairo

Founded where the Nile valley widens into the flat, fertile delta, Cairo has been at the centre of Egyptian life for 1,000 years. It's the largest city in Africa (pop. 13 million), and one of the most densely populated places on earth. Here, by the side of the slow, silent-flowing Nile a bewildering multitude of people live together in an intense bustle of activity.

The heart of the modern metropolis lies on the east bank of the Nile and extends onto the two islands of Gezira and Roda. Large luxury hotels rise on the river's banks in this area, and Garden City's cooling greenery stretches along the waterfront. No less than four bridges span the waters between the towering landmark of the Television Building to the north and Roda Island in the south. One of the busiest of these is Tahrir Bridge, which crosses the main branch of the river from Gezira Island to enter the very heart of the city, Tahrir Square.

Microcosm of Cairo's daily life, **Tahrir Square** throbs and rumbles all day long and half the night as well. The tremendous traffic roundabout is a rabbit warren of underground tunnels connecting pedestrian walkways and the metro system (built by the French and still being extended). In the square, pedlars and vendors take up time-honoured battle-stations each morning, waiting for the day's army of potential customers to hurry by. In open spaces here and there, long queues of Cairenes with endless patience wait phlegmatically for overstuffed buses—in which there's often no room for them—to arrive and depart.

Tahrir Square is surrounded by several of Cairo's prestigious institutions: the **Egyptian Museum** (see p. 38), the Ameri-

can University, the Ministry of Foreign Affairs, and the Nile Hilton. Leaving the square, Talaat Harb street leads you to the beginning of Cairo's chic shopping and business street, **Kasr El-Nil.** Cinemas, cafés, restaurants and tea-shops abound in these thoroughfares, providing refuge from the bustle of daytime commerce. At night the main streets are brightly lit and thronged with strollers, window-shoppers, and young people on their way to the theatre or cinema. If the excitement becomes overpowering, escape to the Nile-side promenade of Cairo's Corniche, due west of any point in the city centre.

Islamic Cairo

Wherever you go in Cairo, above the jumble of rooftops rises the fantasy architecture of mosques, domes and minarets. The city preserves a rich tradition of Islamic artistry, and even the darkening caused by time cannot rob these imaginative structures of their charm. Go east from Tahrir Square passing by the large 19th-century Republic (Abdin) Palace to get to Bab el-Kealk Square, and thence through a busy market area to the massive cylindrical

Mightiest of African rivers is the silent soul of modern Cairo.

CENTRAL CAIRO

CITADEL

Mosque of Mohammed Ali

EL-KHALIFA

Rifai Mosque

Mosque of Mohammed Ali

Midan Salah El-Din

El-Qalaa

Sultan Hassan Mosque

Gayer-Anderson House

El-Nasriya

Sh. Port-Said

Ahmed Ibn Tulun Mosque

Sh. Saliba El-Hod

N

Sh. El-Barrani

Sh. El-Mansur

Sh. El-Saadi

Ruined Aqueduct

Sh. El-Oyun

Sh. Salah Salem

Sh. Balian

Mosque of Amr Ibn El-Asi

Site of El-Fustat

Sh. Kasr El-Aini

Sh. Mari Guirgis

OLD CAIRO

Abu Serga Church

Church of Saint Barbara

El-Moallaqah

Garden City

Sh. El-Corniche

Coptic Museum

Gezirah Sheraton Hotel

Manial Palace

Roda

Sh. El-Roda

Sh. El-Corniche

Fountain

Méridien Hotel

Papyrus Institute

Cairo Sheraton Hotel

Nilometre (El-Miqyas)

Kubry El-Gama

Nile

Kubry El-Giza

Sh. El-Giza

Sh. El-Misaha

Sh. El-Nil

Sh. Murad

Zoo

PIRAMIDS, ALEXANDRIA, EL-FAYOUM

LUXOR, UPPER EGYPT

0   200   400   600 m
0   200   400   600 yards

Sh. = Street
Midan = Square
Kubry = Bridge
● = Nile Bus stop

bastions of **Bab Zuweila,** an imposing gate in Cairo's medieval city walls. Many a condemned criminal or opponent of the ruler was hanged from this gate in times past.

The two minarets on top of the gate actually belong to the adjoining **mosque,** finished in 1420 by the Mameluke Sultan El-Moayyad. This sultan's political enemies had him held prisoner in Bab Zuweila's infamous prison. While he was there he swore to build a mosque if he ever got free of them. When he did, he designed a particularly beautiful one which has outstanding stonework and a pretty garden in its courtyard. Have the caretaker show you the *segn* (prison), and the stairway to the top of Bab Zuweila—there's a marvellous view.

Continue north on Muizz lidini-llah to **Madrassa of Al Ghuri** and the **Tomb of Al Ghuri.** This splendid group —madrassa, mausoleum and wakala—was built by the last-but-one Mameluk sultan, Qansuh Al-Ghuri. The madrassa on the west has a covered cruciform plan and an unusual rectangular minaret with fine "chimney pots" on top. The mausoleum opposite has lost its dome and is now used as a local cultural centre.

The whole group appears in the 1839 painting by David Roberts, "The Silk Bazaar". The Tomb of Al Ghuri, known as "Al Ghuri Palace", has been restored and is open to the public, with art exhibitions and a free folklore evening every Wednesday and Saturday, featuring a Whirling Dervish. It is popular with tourists and locals alike.

From here, walk north a few steps and turn right to reach the **Wakalat Al Ghuri,** a merchant's hostel built in the 16th century, which is open to the public and has arts and crafts on show and on sale. Shortly afterwards, turn left to come to **El-Azhar Mosque and University,** Islam's most prestigious place of learning. Its Arabic name means "The Splendid", and there can be little doubt that its lofty gates and fairytale minarets capture the essence of Islamic architectural bravura. Begun in 970, the original Mosque of Fatima ez-Zahra was later expanded with libraries, hostels for pilgrims and students, gates and minarets. Pass through the sunny courtyard, lined with hostel rooms

Slender minaret thrusts heavenwards, marking a Cairo mosque. When visiting, remove your shoes.

(rwak) to the Great Chamber in order to look at the two prayer niches. El-Azhar is still a university as in medieval times, but today some 30,000 students from all over the Islamic world come here to study medicine and law as well as theology.

Cross the tumultuous traffic in El-Azhar Street to reach Cairo's renowned handicraft bazaar, **Khan el-Khalili.** A shopping trip to Khan el-Khalili is a must for any visitor to Egypt (see also page 84), and yet this is not a tourist market in a strict sense. The tiny shops, selling everything from priceless oriental jewellery to cheap gimcracks and household items, are thronged with Cairenes as well as visitors. Of course, like everywhere, good items have to be sought after; there are plenty of worthless

What would your friends say if you brought a hubble-bubble pipe home?

articles, fakes, forgeries and factory-produced items.

Many of the shops are themselves works of art, boasting ornate doorways of carved wood and delicate traceries, floors covered in oriental carpets, and interiors perfumed with the scent of cedar, sandalwood or incense. Ask the shopkeeper for a tour of his workshops, and he will lead you on a labyrinthine chase to a crumbling room at rooftop level where men and boys are hard at work. Intricate inlay work, pounded copper, or jewelled arabesques in silver or gold are produced before your eyes. When you see what is involved in making one of these handicraft items, you'll realize the prices are quite moderate.

Return to Muizz lidini-llah to get to the imposing **Kalawun Mosque** complex, including a *maristan* (hospital), *madrassa* (theological seminary), the mausoleum of Sultan Kalawun, and the mosque itself. The complex was finished in 1293. Its façade is richly worked in the Islamic style, but somehow curiously reminiscent of Crusader architecture brought from France. Be sure to visit the **Sultan's Mausoleum.** At the end of a dingy passageway, a right turn reveals a magnificent towering portal leading to a great chamber of breathtaking beauty. The carved and gilded ceiling is particularly fine, an outstanding example of the Moslem craftsman's art.

In the adjoining building, rivalling Sultan Kalawun's pomp, is the **Madrassa of Sultan Berquq** dating from 1386. As you pass the finely worked bronze doors, follow a hallway and turn right through another set of bronze doors. You'll find yourself gazing up at a canopy covered in gold arabesques on an azure background. Give the caretaker a small tip, and he'll open a door for you to see the nicely decorated tomb of Sultan Berquq's daughter.

Though it's only a short stroll from Berquq's Madrassa to your next stop, the Musafirkhana, a guide is essential to lead you through the maze of narrow streets. Ask any neighbourhood child—he'll be only too pleased to help. **Musafirkhana** (from the Turkish for "guest house") is a well-preserved mansion built in Mameluke style towards the end of the 18th century. The intricately carved ceiling in the main salon is strikingly attractive.

Find your way back to Muizz lidini-llah to see the restored **El-Aqmar Mosque** (1125), with its unusual façade. A few steps north and to the right is **Bayt es-Suheimi,** home of a **31** sheik who was rector of El-Azhar two centuries ago. His house was divided into the traditional sections of *salamlik*, where male guests were received, and *haramlik*, the private family quarters in which his wife and daughters lived. Off the main reception room is a chamber with huge chairs—symbols of the sheik's importance. Upstairs in the *haramlik*, stained glass, Turkish tiles, and the turned wooden screens *(mousharabiyeh)* change the women's "prison" into a palace.

Approaching the northern wall of medieval Cairo, the great **Mosque of El-Hakim** stands out on the right. The mosque was finished in 1013 by the infamous mad caliph, El-Hakim. It has recently been largely rebuilt and restored by the Bahari Moslem sect, and is still a vast and impressive building.

Nearby, the gates of Bab Futuh and Bab en-Nasr were part of the **city walls** constructed at the end of the 11th century. These early walls have been much mended and rebuilt over the years, but principally by Napoleon's troops less than two centuries ago. The names which soldiers carved into the stones of the towers and bastions can still be read. A guide will appear from nowhere to sell you a ticket, lead you up to the top of the wall, and show you where the town's defenders performed the devilishly effective task of pouring boiling oil down on the heads of attackers.

The Citadel

From the center of Cairo, the approach to the Citadel is between two very noteworthy mosques. **Sultan Hassan Mosque** was a triumphal achievement for its royal builder, who finished it in 1362. The extreme height and austere grandeur of the main portal are matched inside by four cavernous *liwans* (raised prayer areas) inspired by the Persian-Turkish tradition. The **Tomb of Sultan Hassan**, behind the *mihrab* (prayer niche), has pretty stained glass windows, a band of inscription along its walls, and striking squinches supporting the dome. The tomb itself is of Egyptian alabaster. Important restoration is underway, which does not facilitate visiting.

Across the road, the **Rifai Mosque** was finished in 1912 and used as a final resting-place for scions of the house of Mohammed Ali.

Sultan Hassan Mosque: a fountain provides for ritual ablutions.

Take the road up to the **Citadel,** a Crusader-style fortress dating from the time of Saladin (1207). As you pass through the mammoth walls, think of what it must have been like for the Mameluke notables who came to "dine" at Mohammed Ali's invitation in 1811. That night the Pasha sat down to dinner alone knowing full well that all his rivals had been quietly and efficiently dispatched a few hours earlier (see p. 21).

The most eye-catching of the Citadel's buildings is the **Mosque of Mohammed Ali** ("Alabaster Mosque"). The style is Ottoman Baroque, with a few dashes of Louis Philippe. The mosque's plan is Turkish, with a large open forecourt surrounded by a colonnade. Even the pharaohs did not use alabaster as lavishly as Mohammed Ali did: the whole interior is covered in the creamy stone, though the Pasha had his own tomb (to the right as you enter) made from Carrara marble.

Go around behind the mosque when you leave it for a **panoramic view** of Cairo and the Nile. If it's not too hazy, you'll see the pyramids in the distance, poised at the edge of the desert. Before leaving this observation spot, search the jumble of city blocks for the large square court and ziggurat minaret of Ibn Tulun Mosque, a short distance west of the Citadel. It's your next stop.

Though a few Cairo mosques may be older, **Ahmed Ibn Tulun's** is the best-preserved of the city's very early (879) Islamic structures. Its court is the

largest in Cairo, enclosed by a deep porch held up by five arcades. Next door to the mosque is one of Cairo's most fascinating museums, **Gayer-Anderson House,** a pair of traditional Arab houses joined together and filled with works of art both oriental and western. Major Gayer-Anderson, a British officer, bought these two houses (which date from 1540 and 1631), restored them, and lived here between the World Wars.

Blend of ancient and modern—the view from Ibn Tulun Mosque.

Besides being splendid examples of traditional domestic architecture, the museums are a good place to see Persian, Turkish, Arabic, European, and even Chinese decorative arts. The Islamic Museum administers Gayer-Anderson House, which is open during normal museum hours (see p. 116).

(see p. 116)

Sand-colour by day, Cairo blazes in polychrome brilliance at night; Landmark tower is El-Borg, Gezira.

Old Cairo

Old Cairo is a few miles south of the modern city's centre, reachable by taxi or—if you don't mind a bit of crowding—by Nile River Bus from the jetty between Television Tower and Ramses Hilton to the terminus at Masr el-Qadeema (Old Cairo).

Long before the founding of modern Cairo, it was here that the Romans had a fortress called Babylon. The entrance to the old city is between two

bulky Roman towers. Once inside the walls, you are surrounded by Coptic churches and monasteries dating back to the time when Egypt was a Christian country. **El-Moalla-qah**, "The Suspended Church", gets its unusual name from being built on top of two towers of a Roman city gate with its mid-part "suspended" between them. Its foundations date from the 7th century but evidence seems to suggest that there was a church here even in the 4th century. It claims to be the oldest church in Egypt, but then so does **Abu Serga Church.** At the latter, according to legend, Mary, Joseph and the infant Jesus took shelter during their flight into Egypt. Abu Serga is deep in the back streets of Old Cairo which are lined with venerable doorways and paved with big stone blocks smoothed by centuries of wear. Glance upward as you walk along, and behind the *mousharabiyeh* screens on the windows you'll notice at least a dozen pairs of eyes watching your every movement with fascination and delight.

Just a few steps from Abu Serga is the **Church of Saint Barbara,** decorated in typical Coptic style. Next door to it on the right is the small **Synagogue Ben-Ezra.** The caretaker is proud of his little-known house of worship, and will show you the congregation's very old holy books if you contribute to the upkeep of the synagogue.

Before leaving Old Cairo, pay a visit to the **Coptic Museum** (see page 40).

Two Islands

To escape from the exhausting frenzy of the city's busy streets, head for **Gezira** with its sporting clubs, parks and the **Cairo Tower** (El-Borg). A pretty tea-garden at the tower's base is just right for a rest and a refreshing cool drink. Afterwards, whisk to the top of the 600-foot tower for a marvellous view from the observation deck, and perhaps a dish of ice-cream at the snack bar on the floor below. Take your camera, and pick a clear day for your visit.

Roda Island, slightly smaller than Gezira, contains in its northern reaches the **Manial Palace,** now a museum (see page 41). Also in the north is the Meridien Hotel, while at the southern tip you'll be able to see Cairo's **Nilometre** (El-Miqyas), set up in the year 715 to give a clear indication of when the river would be at full flood. Now, due to the Aswan High Dam's careful control of the Nile's waters, the Nilometre has become obsolete. **37**

Museums

Situated in the centre of Cairo, just north of Tahrir Square, the **Egyptian Museum** is one of the most important in the country. Constructed in the middle of the 19th century by the *khedive* Abbas Hilmi, its purpose was to house the wealth of artefacts discovered as a result of the wave of enthusiasm for Egyptology, started off by the French military and cultural invasion. Today, the museum preserves a scholarly character and Egyptologists love it: every single piece is on display and bears a catalogue number. The vastness of the collection is such that, if time is short, it's advisable to concentrate on the best items rather than trying to see everything fleetingly.

Turn left after handing in your ticket and walk between pairs of colossal statues to the Old Kingdom Room harbouring the most ancient statues and sarcophagi. A small funerary chamber from Dahshur (Desheri, 6th Dynasty) has colourful engraved walls on which are noted the supplies provided for the dead man on his celestial voyage, including a few jugs of beer to quench a powerful Egyptian thirst.

Farther along, you'll be struck by the stylized but still intensely life-like statue (No. 141) of a scribe from Saqqara (5th Dynasty), its glass eyes catching glints of light with startling reality. In Room 32, the realistic statues of High Priest Ra-Hotep and his wife Nofret (No. 223) are plain evidence that the ancient Egyptians were very beautiful, and knew how to make the most of their gifts with cosmetics and clothing. The artists' magic was not reserved exclusively for humans, as No. 446 (in Room 12) proves: the beautifully serene cow effigy is a symbol of the goddess Hathor. It was found "living" in the shed behind it, which comes complete with its own starry firmament. In Room 8, the gilded coffin lid set with carnelians and blue glass was made for Tutankhamon's brother. Room 3, devoted to the reign of Akhenaton, has two giant statues of the king in the exaggerated naturalistic style of the period, showing a distended belly and enormous effeminate thighs. They are grotesque but impressive.

Above the west stairs you can visit the War-and-Peace Exhibition, artfully arranged in a large room. Some of the most interesting artefacts come from the reign of Ramesis II, including a huge stone block representing the king's fist, a symbol of the weight of pharaoh's authority. Other pieces include the finely painted chest of Tutankhamon, the coffin of Ramesis II, treasure cases and some beautiful items from Amarna.

For a look at the daily activities of ancient Egyptians, Rooms 22, 27, 32 and 37 are the ones to visit. The delightful little wooden figures which fill these rooms were made as "servants" for the dead, to provide for the honoured departed in the next life. Soldiers, boatmen with a funeral ship, craftsmen with toy tools, even ducks, fish, dogs and cattle—whole villages of wooden figures—were found all together. Daily life along the Nile in pharaonic times was obviously busy and varied, whether in this world or the next.

Prepare yourself for a thrill when you enter the section specially reserved for the display of **King Tutankhamon's treasures.** The king died mysteriously at the tender age of 19 years. His half-finished tomb in the Valley of the Kings at Thebes (Luxor) was filled with an array of treasure unparalleled in its variety, exquisite beauty, and sheer weight of gold. Seeing this treasure of

King Tut's funeral mask: a flawless treasure for a minor king.

1,700 items buried with an unimportant king, who can even imagine what the tombs of great and long-lived pharaohs such as Ramesis II must have contained? But only Tutankhamon's escaped the ravages brought by centuries of grave-robbing, to be found intact in 1922 by a British archaeologist named Howard Carter.

In Room 4 are the best of the "smaller" pieces, including a solid gold coffin, much jewellery, and Tutankhamon's famous mask, considered by many to be one of the most beautiful objects in the world. The treasure fills the corridors and galleries near Room 4 as well: gold-plated cases, one of them large enough to garage a small car; the king's exquisite bejewelled golden throne, bearing the sun-symbol of Aton (whom the king later forsook, turning back to worship of Amon); and a large golden box surmounted by rows of sacred cobras *(uraeus)* and guarded by four comely gilded maidens. When you visit Tutankhamon's tomb in the Valley of the Kings (see p. 72), you will marvel that all this treasure could have been fitted into such a small underground room.

Just off Bab el-Kealk Square next to the Egyptian Library, is the **Museum of Islamic Art.** You'll be surprised at the variety of things made by Moslem craftsmen, including fine prayer mats, stained glass, inlaid stone work, mosque lamps, faience and illuminated manuscripts. The arms collection alone is worth visiting to see rifles and siege guns worked in silver, daggers and swords set with precious stones, and deadly-looking poignards, scimitars and yataghans. Remember as you tour the collections that Moslem artists were forbidden by the Koran to portray any being with a soul. Obviously, there were lapses in the strict observance of this rule.

Centrepiece of Old Cairo is the **Coptic Museum.** Fine examples of Coptic craftsmanship found in old churches and houses have been assembled here, especially carved wood, stained glass, *mousharabiyeh* screens and sculpted works. At first it looks very similar to Islamic work: the same delicate tracery used to illuminate Moslem holy books is found in Coptic Bibles as well. But the difference is soon apparent. Christian craftsmen were allowed by their religion to portray men and beasts. Coptic art is Egyptian Islamic art with the prohibitions removed and the artist unfettered.

Cairo's Museum of Islamic Art: a permanent collection open to all.

Prince Mohammed Ali's palace on Roda Island became a museum after the fall of the monarchy. In the **Manial Palace Museum,** you'll find pavilions and salons filled with the luxuries and curiosities of royal daily life, from lustrous Turkish tiles and carpets to sparkling jewels and chandeliers. With its beautiful gardens, the Manial Palace complex is a pleasant refuge from the noise and dust of the city. Its ancient walls now shelter a hotel facility, where you can get lunch or dinner for the price of a ticket.

At Professor Hassan Ragab's **Papyrus Institute,** in a houseboat on the Nile near the Sheraton Hotel, you can see papyrus being made and buy the finished product bearing a painting or drawing. One kilometre further south is **Dr. Ragab Pharaonic Village** on Jacob Island. A barge-like floating "amphitheatre" is towed round a winding, papyrus-fringed canal, giving interesting glimpses of agricultural and industrial work being done in the ancient Egyptian style.

For museum opening hours see page 116.

Excursions from Cairo

Pyramids of Giza

The route to the pyramids of Giza lies along the appropriately named Avenue of the Pyramids. The road is usually congested but Giza's wonders of the world soon come into view behind hotels, offices, and apartment buildings. Empress Eugenie of France was the first to admire this view of the pyramids when she inaugurated the Avenue in 1869. She had come to Egypt for the opening of the Suez Canal.

The pyramids are right at the edge of the modern city, and also right on the verge of the desert. The geometrical shapes, so perfect from a distance, yield their secrets of construction as you approach them. Each is made from millions of massive stone blocks, and their faces are in fact like giant staircases, not smooth, as they first appear to be. With no doors or windows to give them scale, the monolithic forms seem deceptively small until you arrive at their bases. Then, these man-made mountains completely overpower you with their ponderous, precise majesty.

The **Great Pyramid of Cheops,** largest of the three, is 450 feet (137 metres) high and is made of nearly 2½ million gigantic stone blocks. Many visitors are tempted to clamber to the top of this impressive monument for a better look at the city and the Nile, but this gymnastic feat is both extremely dangerous and forbidden. As for a visit to the interior of the Great Pyramid, only the fairly athletic and non-claustrophobic should follow the guide into the spooky depths for a look at Cheops' funerary chamber, complete with sarcophagus and ventilation shafts.

Camel-drivers in the area are ever-ready to hoist you onto their ungainly beasts—who kneel obligingly—for the short ride between pyramids. For those who prefer comfort to adventure, several horse-drawn carriages are also available for hire.

The **Pyramid of Chephren** is actually only a foot or two lower than the Great Pyramid, but as it's built on higher ground it looks taller from a distance. The covering of smooth-finished stones, once a feature of almost all the pyramids, can still be seen near the top. You can penetrate into the heart of this man-made mountain too, but do so only with a guide.

Pyramids

The ideas that first prompted the ancient Egyptians to start burying their dead under mounds are shrouded in the mystery of time. But whatever the original motives, from these first early piles of earth covered in bricks, some of the most astounding structures ever constructed by man came to be developed. (It is said that 100,000 men laboured for 20 years to build the Great Pyramid of Cheops.)

The earliest tombs *(mastabas)* were rectangular and flat-topped. When Imhotep put several *mastabas* on top of one another for King Zoser's tomb, the idea caught on and the era of pyramid construction began. Many of the mammoth monuments seem uncomplicated in their basic architecture (see below). In fact, the simplicity conceals a whole world of intricate design intimately related to the religious beliefs of the early Egyptians.

Pyramid of Cheops

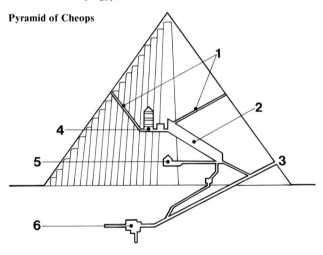

1. Shafts	**4.** King's chamber
2. Gallery	**5.** Queen's chamber
3. Entrance	**6.** Underground chamber

The third and smallest **Pyramid of Menkure** (Mykerinos) is 204 feet (66 metres) high and was the last of the three Giza pyramids to be built. Notice the temples and tombs called *mastabas,* built all around the three great pyramids. They were put here so family, friends and noble servants of the pharaohs could be near their sovereign. All this impressive building was done in the times of the Old Kingdom's 4th Dynasty, about 2600 B.C. Other pyramids, earlier and later, line the Nile,

Stele tells of early repairs to world's most enigmatic monument.

but those of Cheops, Chephren and Menkure are acknowledged as the finest.

The **Sphinx**—Abu el-Houl, or "Father of Fear" in Arabic—was sculpted in the image of Pharaoh Chephren as a guard for his pyramidal tomb. Some 1,000 years after the Sphinx was made, the ever-shifting desert sands had covered it completely. Thutmose IV (1425-08 B.C.) cleared the sand away and restored the great beast, according to an inscription on a stele which stands between its paws. After another 3,000 years the Mamelukes used the monument as a target for gunnery practice, thereby carrying out the Islamic prohibition against graven images while simultaneously improving the skills of their cannoneers. Recently, times have turned in the Sphinx's favour, and it is very well looked after by the Department of Antiquities.

Near the Sphinx, the **Funerary Temple of Chephren** is remarkable for the size and smoothness of its granite blocks and for its floor, made of alabaster. Another curiosity in the pyramid complex is the **solar barque,** one of several long-boats made of Lebanese cedar which were buried in deep pits next to the Great Pyramid. The boat, meant for use by Cheops on his celestial journey to the Other World, is kept in a small museum on the southern side of the Great Pyramid.

Saqqara and Memphis

Skirting fields watered by canals from the Nile, the road south from Giza leads to **Saqqara,** the largest necropolis in Egypt, with hundreds of tombs and monuments erected throughout ancient Egyptian history. Activity here was especially intense during the Old Kingdom, when pharaohs had their capital at Memphis, close by.

Look first at the **Step Pyramid of Zoser** (or Jeser, 3rd Dynasty) the very earliest of the great pyramids built perhaps a century before those at Giza. King Zoser's architect, a nobleman named Imhotep, put all his ingenuity to work when designing this memorable tomb for his royal patron. Originally called *mastabas*, Egyptian tombs were rectangles more or less modified to suit the tastes and budget of the builder and future occupant. But Imhotep stacked six large *mastabas* of diminishing size on top of one another to create the Step Pyramid. The idea was a great success and a later king, Seneferou (4th Dynasty), also had a pyramid **45** constructed at Dahshur, visible from Saqqara to the south. Seneferou's pyramid abandoned steps in favour of a standard base capped with a small, roof-like pyramidal top. This combination produces a bottom-heavy visual effect making the pyramids sides look "bent" when viewed from below. It was Seneferou's son Cheops who perfected the design and constructed the most impressive pyramid of all at Giza.

Near Giza pyramids, a son follows in his father's footsteps. Right: Kagemni Tomb, Saqqara.

Of the tombs surrounding the Step Pyramid, several are graced with murals of exceptional beauty. The **mastaba of Princess Idut** (6th Dynasty) is at the end of the colonnade which you approach just after buying your entry ticket. It is particularly rich in nautical scenes. Next to it is the small **Pyramid of Unas** (5th Dynasty), and visible in the distance from this point are the Dahshur pyramids, including Seneferou's "bent" one.

North-east of the Step Pyramid, the **Tomb of Mereruka** (6th Dynasty) has 30 rooms decorated with scenes of hunting and fishing so exact in their detail that zoologists could use them to study the wildlife of ancient Egypt. The **Tomb of Kagemni** (6th Dynasty), next to that of Mereruka, has a number of equally fine murals, but with more of the colour preserved.

A short drive or walk to the north-west of the Step Pyramid brings you to the modest Rest-House named after Auguste Mariette, the French Egyptologist who discovered many of the monuments in this area. Camel-drivers will trot you from the Rest-House across the sands on their beasts (or you can walk the short distance) to the **Tomb of Ti** (5th Dynasty).

This most breathtakingly beautiful of Old Kingdom tombs was buried by desert sands for 4,500 years until uncovered by the ever-curious Mariette. Lord Ti was a high court official under several pharaohs, a powerful man who chose the finest craftsmen and artists to embellish his tomb.

Just north of Ti's tomb, you see the **Serapeium,** also discovered by Mariette in 1850–51. Sacred bulls were buried here from the earliest period of Egyptian civilization right up to the time of Christianity.

On the way back to Cairo, you can detour to the ruins of **Memphis** on the Nile, though there is little left of the great metropolis which remained the first city of Egypt until the end of the 6th Dynasty (about 2200 B.C.). A colossal, recumbent limestone statue of Ramesis II and an alabaster sphinx—which actually date from New Kingdom times—are all that recall ancient Memphis. The gigantic red granite statue of Ramesis II which once stood here is now next to the railway station in Cairo's Ramesis Square.

Alexandria
(Pop. 3,000,000)

About 220 kilometres from Cairo is Alexandria, accessible by road, rail and air. Founded by Alexander the Great in 332 B.C., this city has lived through momentous times, though today little is left of its greatness except memories. Modern buildings crowd and cover antique ruins, and the polyglot internationalism of the 19th-century Levantine port has all but faded away.

Many Cairenes spend part of their summer holidays in this attractive Mediterranean resort, or at the nearby beaches of Al Agami.

You can easily visit Alexandria's sights in a day, or you can spend a couple of nights in one of the many hotels. Start at the western end of the sweeping

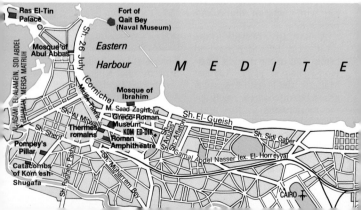

Corniche named 26 July Street. It's the main waterfront thoroughfare and surrounds the eastern harbour. The coast road continues from the centre of town all the way to Montazah Palace 8 kilometres to the east. The peninsula at the Corniche's western end holds the former royal palace of Ras El-Tin.

Just east of the palace, part of the 15th-century Fort of Qait Bey, now serving as a Naval Museums, stands on the alleged site of Alexandria's ancient Pharos the elaborate lighthouse which was one of the wonders of the ancient world. Today, there's nothing left of the lighthouse which flashed its warning in the age of the Ptolemies.

South of the Qait Bey Fort just a block from the Corniche stands the **Mosque of Abul Ab-bas** (1767), Alexandria's most impressive. Continue to the centre of town to find **Tahrir Square.** Though this is the city's largest public square, it's less important to tramway-riders, bus passengers and café-sitters than **Saad Zaghloul Square** a few blocks farther east. Zaghloul Square is the place for all these activities, as well as being the bus terminus.

Turn inland for a visit to the **Greco-Roman Museum.** Despite its name, it holds a good number of pharaonic relics as well. Other fascinating reminders of the city's Greek and Roman past are the Roman amphitheatre at Kom ed-Dikka, unearthed in 1963, and the nearby catacombs of Kom esh-Shugafa. The catacombs date from the early years of the Christian era, and preserve an

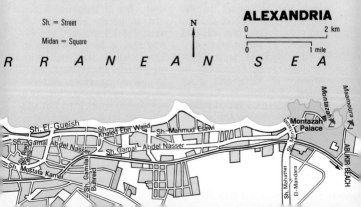

unusual mixture of pharaonic and Roman styles. Nearby **Pompey's Pillar** has nothing to do with the redoubtable General Pompey. The 98-foot-high monument of rosy Aswan granite was erected for Emperor Diocletian in the 3rd century A.D., considerably after Pompey's time. Continuing east, don't miss the Jewellery Museum in **Zizinia.** Previously a royal palace, it now houses an impressive collection of the jewels of the former royal family of Egypt.

Alexandria's beaches start in the centre of town, but the best are those to the east at **Maamoura, Montazah** and **Abukir.** This last, at the site of Nelson's victory over Napoleon's fleet in 1798, is now famous for its seafood restaurants.

West of Alexandria, the Mediterranean coast stretches some 500 kilometres to the Libyan frontier. There are several resorts along the way, all accessible by public transport. A particularly popular Egyptian resort, now practically an extension of Alexandria, is AL AGAMI. Beyond is EL-ALAMEIN, which took on immense importance during the savage battles of 1942. Here you'll find a museum and vast cemeteries of war-dead from both **50** sides. SIDI ABDEL RAHMAN,

20 kilometres beyond the town, has a beautiful beach and a hotel. Even further west, 185 kilometres from El-Alamein, is MERSA MATRUH. This town busies itself with provincial government matters, desert commerce and Mediterranean fishing, but you can devote yourself to sun and sea.

The desert road between Alexandria and Cairo has little traffic and offers the opportunity of visiting the **Coptic**

monasteries in Wadi Natrun. After following the road 120 kilometres from Alexandria, turn right at the Rest-House to reach the monasteries, 10 kilometres from the main road.

High walls, great piety, and a simple, ascetic life are the things valued by the monks at the four monasteries of Deir Amba Bishoi, Deir es-Suryani, Deir Amba Baramos, and Deir Abu Makar. This last was the most important of the ancient monasteries, giving the Coptic

Flags, fiacres and multilingual signs: nostalgic reminders of Alexandria's polyglot history.

church most of its early fathers. Monks have lived in seclusion here since the 4th century. Recent excavations have disclosed a skull-less skeleton thought by some to be that of St. John the Baptist (his head is in the Omayyad Mosque in Damascus). Visitors are welcome to tour certain parts of the monasteries. **51**

Fayyoum

Fayyoum is a large area of cultivation irrigated by a canal from the Nile and surrounded by the Western Desert, less than two hours' drive from Cairo.

The land in the Fayyoum area is flat, with lush fields tilled by bullock-drawn plough or men wielding primitive mattocks. Horsecarts piled high with cane, grass mats, fodder or passengers rumble over the roads, passing women swathed in flowing black robes with heavily laden baskets balanced expertly on their heads. Here and there a palm grove provides welcome shade, or a picturesque waterwheel of darkened wood creaks slowly around.

Medinet El-Fayyoum, capital city of the province, is a considerable town of some 400,000 people. Crocodilopolis was its name in former times as it was sacred to the crocodile-god Sobek.

Qaroun, a large lake in the north of Fayyoum, is well-stocked with fish and is famous for hunting and duck shooting. The late King Farouk's old hunting lodge on the southern shore has been converted into a hotel.

Of the pharaonic sites in Fayyoum, **Medinet Madi** is the best preserved but is difficult to get to; the pyramids at Meidum, Lauhoun and Hawara are more accessible, but the most convenient site to visit is **Kom Oushim,** on the escarpment overlooking the Fayyoum just off the Cairo–Fayyoum desert road, where there are the remains of the Ptolomaic/Roman town of Karanis. There is an interesting museum here.

Venerable monks at Wadi Natrun have lived in pious austerity since Christianity began. Below: Fayyoum, a vast desert garden.

Upper Egypt

As the slender green valley of the Nile meanders ever southwards, the Egypt of the Arabs is left behind giving way to the Egypt of the Africans. Lower Egypt's delta is vast and rich, but in Upper Egypt the fertile soil brought (until the building of the Aswan High Dam) by the mighty river, lines only a few hundred yards along either bank. The *fellahin* (peasant farmers) make up for the lack of land by intensive cultivation of the little they have. A journey south along the Nile here reveals green fields of sugarcane and cotton, with cows pulling primitive ploughs, turning waterwheels, or towing carts. Every sort of pumping system ever devised by man, simple or ingenious, is pressed into service to irrigate the fields.

Dotted along the Nile's banks are traces of pharaonic Egypt, from dusty heaps of broken pottery to magnificent temples. At **Abydos,** the votive **temple** to Osiris built by Seti I (19th Dynasty) has fine mural paintings, though you must step carefully in the shadowy rooms with their broken floors. (Bring a powerful light if you have one.) Abydos was a place especially sacred to the memory of Osiris, the well-loved earthly god who was murdered and cut into pieces by his brother. Unable to rule on earth, Osiris became king of the nether world. The sacred city built here in his honour disappeared long ago, but the great Seti temple remains an imposing monument to him.

The **Osireion,** behind the temple, was a cenotaph for Seti I, who wanted to show his love of Osiris by having a tomb here, though he arranged for his true burial to be in the Valley of the Kings at Thebes.

Farther on, a five-minute walk across the sand brings you to the ruined **Temple of Ramesis II,** which still shows some traces of the bright colours which once blazed from its walls.

Continuing southeast along the river you come to the temple complex at **Denderah** (Tentyris). Although the principal monument there today is the Ptolemaic temple, Denderah was a sacred site from historic times. The **Mammisi* of Augustus** to the right after passing through the great gate, was built in Roman times. The artistry of the reliefs is poor compared with the excellence of Middle and New Kingdom art. The fascinating scenes on the south

----

* birth-temple

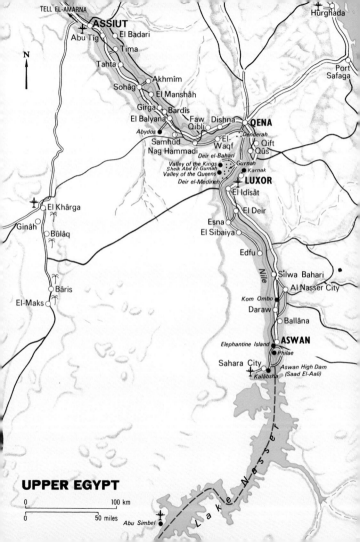

wall and throughout the temple show the birth and nourishment of an infant god, meant to symbolize the Egyptian monarch. Another birth-temple, the Mammisi of Nectanebo (30th Dynasty) was built late in pharaonic times. Between the two Mammisi are the ruins of a Coptic church.

A pharaoh's life was filled with dazzling ceremony. Here he greets Hathor and Horus (Denderah).

Denderah's **main temple** is dedicated to Hathor, mother of the gods, wife of Horus. She is often portrayed as a beautiful woman whose head is topped by a pair of graceful horns bordering a solar disc. Sometimes she takes the shape of a fertile, genial cow, and sometimes she combines attributes of both woman and cow. The columns in the hypostyle hall are topped by capitals bearing the face of Hathor. The offertory hall has similar columns and in the

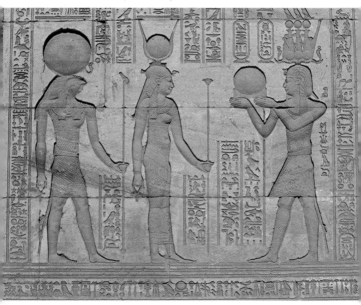

murals Hathor is shown going about her benevolent business. Farther into the temple, the dingy and mysterious holy of holies is sombre and vaguely disquieting as you stand surrounded by mystical bas-reliefs and the dust of ages. The caretaker will take you down into the crypts for a look at several fine murals, but don't go if you're averse to stooping and scrambling, or to sharing the claustrophobic underground tunnels with bats.

Above the holy of holies are rooms with murals showing the Egyptian process of embalming, and ceilings framed by the sinuous body of the celestial goddess Nut, who symbolized the sky to ancient Egyptians. Up on the temple roof, the bright sunlight dispels the gloom of the holy of holies at once. Look for the Sacred Lake on the temple's western side. Behind the temple is the smaller Temple of Isis, sister and wife of Osiris and mother of Horus.

Divine Coexistence

Ancient Egypt's religion was a matter of divine profusion and confusion. Scores of local gods merged attributes with one another and with gods from other areas, and no one was ever quite sure which was which. All appear to have been happy and benevolent, and early Egyptians seem to have felt no pressing need to tidy up the pantheon. The simplified chart below may help you identify some of the most popular gods.

Deity	Forms	Function
Amon-Ra	Sun, ram, hawk	Chief god, patron of Thebes
Osiris	Pharaoh	Underworld god
Isis	Beautiful woman	Sister-wife of Osiris; Horus' mother
Hathor	Cow, goddess with horns	Fertility, love, joy
Horus	Falcon, winged solar disc, infant	Sun god, protector of the king; many other functions of deity
Anubis	Jackal	Funeral ceremonies god
Thoth	Ibis	Wisdom and learning
Ptah	Man	Creator, teacher of skills and crafts
Maat	Ostrich plume	Justice

Luxor

(Pop. 60,000)

From 2100 to 750 B.C. (the 10th to 25th Dynasties) the centre of Egyptian power and glory was focused in the temples of Luxor and Karnak in the city of Thebes. It was here that the New Kingdom (1570–1100 B.C.) saw its finest hour. While the city of the dead lay on the western bank of the Nile, the city of the living thrived between the two great temples.

But the fourteen centuries of Theban grandeur were brought abruptly to an end by the Assyrian invasion of Egypt in the 7th century B.C. and Thebes soon became only a crumbling but magnificent attraction for visiting Greeks and, later, Romans.

Then, renewed interest in the city saw Egyptologists sweeping away the dust of centuries from Theban temples and seeking

No adventure leaves lifetime memories like a cruise on the Nile.

the hidden entrances to pharaonic tombs. The mid-19th century opening of the Suez Canal increased European interest in Egypt, and visitors quickly discovered the area's perfect winter climate. Tourists have been enjoying Luxor's temperatures, temples and tombs ever since.

The town's long riverside Corniche is bordered by trees, with Nile cruise boat docks dotted along the bank. Graceful feluccas tie up next to the tourist boats, hoping to take passengers for a waterborne view of the town, or to ferry them to the Valley of the Kings on the Nile's opposite shore. The great pillars of Luxor Temple, illuminated at night, dominate the eastern bank, and strollers staying on the boats or in the renowned Winter Palace Hotel never tire of passing this ancient monument. A week seems like a very short time to spend in this supremely pleasant place—half a week is barely enough to see the essentials.

The most convenient spot to begin your sightseeing is at **Luxor Temple.** This most impressive building served as the setting for only one solemn pageant celebrated at the beginning of each new year, that of the chief god Amon. Amenophis III (18th Dynasty) and Ramesis II (19th Dynasty) contributed most to the construction of the temple during the period 1400–1250 B.C. When you visit it, let your imagination conjure up the ceremonies of Amon's procession, with the god symbolized in various forms—Amon-Ra, the Sun God, or as Amon-Min, the lascivious and outrageously demonstrative deity whose unmistakable phallic image appears in the temple's murals in several places.

In front of the great pylon (gateway) is one of the two finely wrought obelisks, which Mohammed Ali presented to France in 1831. The other was taken to Paris and now stands in the Place de la Concorde. Inside the great pylon up to the left, the little Mosque of Abu'l Haggag is perched on pillars in the court of Ramesis II. Several churches once shared the temple grounds as well. Past this court, a great colonnaded way, simple but enormous, leads to the older, inner court of Amenophis III.

At first it's difficult to imagine that the Luxor Temple was a "minor" one, but the short ride to the awe-inspiring temple in Karnak will bring you face-to-face with pharaonic Egypt's grandest monument of all. The

Great Temple of Amon is actually the largest of a vast complex of temples, sacred lakes, chapels and sphinx-lined triumphal ways which filled nearly two miles along the Nile, from Karnak to the Luxor Temple. A century of archaeological work has uncovered and reconstructed a great deal, but there was so much built during the 1400 years of Theban greatness that the work may never be finished.

The Great Temple was built, modified and expanded according to pharaohs' whims over a period of 2,000 years from the Middle Kingdom to Roman times. The first part you see was the last part built: the towering

and massive **first pylon,** largest in the world, was to have been the Ptolemies' contribution to the temple, but they never finished it. Its broad expanse was never carved to record the great moments of the Ptolemy dynasty. Behind the tremendous bulk of the 40-foot thick pylon is the largest **court** of any

Egyptian temple, an open space of about 8,000 square yards. The Temple of Seti II (19th Dynasty) is the little shrine on the left as you enter. The one farther along on the right is the work of Ramesis III (20th Dynasty). The sacred barque, symbolizing the sun's journey through the celestial "sea" was mounted in a place of honour on the structure in the court's centre.

The second pylon, guarded by two colossal statues of Ramesis II, hides the most stupendous room in the ancient world: the **great hypostyle hall,** overpowering with its 134 gigantic columns, those along the central aisle being even taller than the rest. A surprising amount of the original paint and decoration is visible high up on the columns. Stand here a moment. It takes a period of time for the full effect of this huge room to sink in.

The third pylon, directly behind the great hypostyle hall, dates from the reign of Amenophis III (18th Dynasty, about 1400 B.C.). The narrow court between the third and fourth pylons held four fine granite obelisks, of which only one

In a corner of Karnak Temple, sphinx-like rams bask in the sun. **61**

remains, but an even bigger obelisk (one of a pair) erected past the fourth pylon by Queen Hatsheput is even better. The fourth and fifth pylons, erected by Thutmose I (18th Dynasty, about 1525 B.C.) are among the oldest parts of the temple.

Past the sixth pylon is the granite sanctuary which housed the sacred barques, and behind this is the very oldest section of the great temple, part of a modest shrine erected in Middle Kingdom times.

The ruined temple area is so vast, with piles of stones fallen here and there and hidden by high grass, that most of the structures which used to surround the temple are difficult to identify without an elaborate archaeological plan. But there is no missing the **Sacred Lake** just

Egyptian Temples

Though each great temple is slightly different, all have a similar master-plan. A mammoth gateway, or pylon, came first, and behind it was an open courtyard. A second pylon and a second courtyard followed. Next came a room called a "hypostyle", filled with columns to support a roof. Another such room might follow, sometimes called the hall of offerings. Finally, the inner sanctum, or "holy of holies", was where the god "lived" and where priests performed arcane ceremonies and sacred rites. A typical temple plan might look like this.

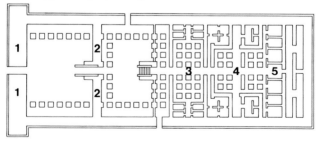

1. First pylon
2. Second pylon
3. Hypostyle hall
4. Hall of offerings
5. Holy of holies

south of the Great Temple of Amon. Part of the ceremonial at Amon's temple required setting the sacred barques afloat on the lake to symbolize the daily celestial journey of Amon-Ra, the Sun. Behind the lake to the east are seats for the evening sound-and-light show. At the northern corner of the Sacred Lake a man at a small and very un-pharaonic stand sells refreshing drinks, providing an excuse for a rest-stop.

In the late afternoon, Luxor's fine little **museum** north of the Etap Hotel opens its doors, and no visitor to Luxor should miss spending a pleasant half-hour in its air-conditioned rooms. Unlike the jumbled Egyptian Museum in Cairo, the Luxor Museum is small and the collection well selected and artfully displayed. The striding basalt statue of Thutmose III (No. 2) is particularly fine, and the striking, unusual sandstone bust of Amenophis IV (Akhenaton, No. 53) gives some appreciation of this exceptional pharaoh's strong character. Notice, too, the gold bracelet that belonged to Queen Nefertiti.

The best time for a stroll in the modern town of Luxor is at dusk, when the market streets are still filled with life but not overcrowded, and most of the day's business has been done.

At sunset, it's pleasant to sit at a Nile-side café. One, with an upper-level terrace, between Luxor Temple and the New Winter Palace Hotel, has a fine view of the river and the temple.

Theban Necropolis

The Valley of the Kings shelters the fabulous tombs of many great Theban pharaohs, including the relatively modest one belonging to Tutankhamon. But the valley is only a small part of a vast "city of the dead" which extends over large tracts on the far (western) side of the Nile from Luxor. Including the tombs of countless nobles, court officers and royal family members, the number of burial-places is in the hundreds. A dozen temples, large and small, are scattered throughout the necropolis. An attempt to appreciate all this magnificence in a single day could well end in bewilderment and exhaustion, so it's a good idea to plan at least two days to tour the major sights of Thebes' City of the Dead.

Motorized ferry-boats ply the Nile between the Winter Palace dock, the Savoy Hotel dock, and the western bank. The boats operate continuously between 6 a.m. and 6 p.m. and you buy a return ticket when **63** you board on the east bank. The booth at the west bank dock is the place to buy your tickets to one or more of the temples and tombs. Don't set off to the tombs without them. Next to the booth, plenty of taxis and donkeys are always available for hire.

From the dock, a road heads inland through lush irrigated farmland. About a mile and a half along, towards the ragged mountains, a pair of mammoth seated figures rise from the midst of a farmer's field: these are the celebrated **Colossi of Memnon.** The temple which must have enclosed them was ruined long ago by earthquakes, but these two seated figures of Pharaoh Amenophis III remain, giving mute testimony to the greatness of their maker more than 3,000 years after his death. Unlike most monuments in this region, the Colossi sit on priceless agricultural land, though the edge of the desert is only a few hundred yards away.

West of the Colossi is a complex of temples called by its modern Arabic name, **Medinet Habu.** A rough and crumbling mud brick wall surrounds two temples which seem, as you enter, to present a never-ending file of pylons. The first temple was started in the time of Amenophis I (18th Dynasty). It's very revealing to compare this small, pretty temple with the much larger one behind it, which is the work of Ramesis III (20th Dynasty), who lived some 350 years after Amenophis. The Ramesis temple was put up all at one time rather than over the centuries, and though its size is impressive, it is less pleasing aesthetically. Look closely at the relief decoration: it's carved very deeply to make it more dramatic, but the depth makes it seem somewhat coarse as well. The temple's plan is the classic one, though it has three hypostyle halls, and cleaning of the decoration revealed a surprising amount of surviving colour.

From Medinet Habu, a road runs directly to the **Valley of the Queens.** Close to 80 tombs here sheltered the remains of queens and royal children, though few have survived the ravages of time in good condition. One is well worth a visit. Number 55, that of Prince Amon-her-Khopeshef (20th Dynasty) preserves fine paintings with astonishingly bright colours, especially the blues and yellows. No. 44, the Tomb of Prince Kha'emwaset, and No. 52 of Queen Tyti, are also open to the public. The finest tomb, that of Queen Neferlari (wife of Ramesis II), No. 66,

is closed while restoration is carried out to repair damage caused by salt deposits.

Returning from the Valley of the Queens, take the first turning left to reach the necropolis of **Deir el Medineh.** Of the hundreds of tombs discovered within and around this modern-day village, No. 1 is of greatest interest. It belonged to Sennejem, a high official of the 19th Dynasty, and its paintings retain an amazing freshness of colour, looking as though they were completed yesterday. Be careful as you descend because the stairway is broken, and the rock-hewn entrance very small. Tomb No. 359, of Inherka (20th

Unusual neighbours? Not for Theban farmers passing by every day.

Dynasty) is very close to No. 1 and is filled with paintings of gorgeous sloe-eyed goddesses.

The kings of the 19th Dynasty were ambitious builders, and none more than Ramesis II (1304–1237 B.C), whose awesome monuments are strewn throughout Egypt. His tomb in the Valley of the Kings is a little disappointing, but the funerary temple he built to his own memory at the edge of the cultivated land remains a stupendous architectural achievement. Called the **Ramesseum,** it was **65**

fine Osiride statues of the pharaoh, to your left. Next is a great bulk of ruined stone which formed a colossus of truly incredible stature: this seated figure was 56 feet high and weighed over 2,200,000 pounds.

Behind the Ramesseum on the hillside is the necropolis called **Sheik Abd El-Gurnah,** after the present-day village there. All the tombs worthy of a visit date back to the 18th Dynasty, one of ancient Egypt's most glorious periods. Be prepared for some delay. The tombs tend to be small but the crowds of visitors are not. Some tombs are lit, but in others caretakers illuminate the tomb interiors by an ingenious juxtaposition of mirrors, reflecting a brilliant beam of sunlight into the darkness. But only a few people can be in one of the tombs at a time or the beam will be blocked. In some smaller tombs numbers are restricted to protect the murals. Tombs are occasionally closed for restoration work.

The **Tomb of Nakht,** No. 52, is small but depicts all the Nile's abundance in its beautiful scenes of wine-making, fruit-gathering, and reaping. Nakht

a vast collection of palaces, temples and storerooms. Now, though much ruined, the scale of the temple and the score of huge statues in the image of Ramesis leave modern visitors with a vivid impression. The present entrance to the ruins takes you into the second **66** court, past four pillars with

Sacred sunlight, put to work with a crude reflector, gives tantalizing glimpses of Theban gentility.

was an astronomer attached to the Temple of Amon. In the nearby **Tomb of Mena,** No. 69, the colours are equally beautiful, though the mirror-light and the glass plates which protect the murals weaken their impact. The **Tomb of Sennefer,** No. 96, is a bit out of the way, half way up the hillside, at the bottom of a steep stairway and through a small opening. However, the extra effort is amply rewarded, as the colours are amazingly well preserved and the uneven ceiling is charmingly decorated with grapevines.

The **Tomb of Rekhmire,** No. 100, is as magnificent as one might expect for an ex-mayor of Thebes. Murals show ambassadors from foreign countries bringing offerings of giraffes, leopards, baboons and monkeys, elephant tusks and produce. Other murals show vignettes of Theban daily life as men work in the fields or at their crafts, producing goods to be offered to the great Amon.

Ramose's Tomb, No. 55, like Rekhmere-Ra's is also an imposing eternal resting-place. But his pharaoh, Amenophis IV (Akhenaton) carried out his religious revolution while work was in progress, and Ramose's tomb was abandoned unfinished when pharaoh and court moved down the Nile to Tell el-Amarna. The bas-reliefs in the tomb are exceptionally fine. Girls with delicate features and carefully plaited hair were carved with great skill, and then abandoned unpainted. The effect is of exquisite engravings rather than of bas-reliefs. A few figures are outlined in black—the first stage in the painting process—and these offer a contrasting beauty.

For yet another glimpse of Theban artistry, find the **Tomb of Khaemhat,** No. 57. Unusually, it shelters several statues of its owner and his family. The nearby tomb of Userhet, No. 56, is also worth a visit.

The artistic brilliance of the 18th Dynasty seen in these tombs stands out even more boldly in the temples of **Deir el-Bahari,** west of the main road. The story of Queen Hatshepsut, for whom one of the temples was originally meant, is a fascinating tale. If a pharaoh had no legitimate son to be his heir, he often put forward one of his illegitimate sons and married him to one of his legitimate daughters, thereby strengthening the son's claim. This happened to Thutmose I, bastard son of Amenophis I. But Thutmose and his wife Ahmose had the same problem over again: no son. Thutmose II was therefore selected from among Thutmose I's numerous bastard sons, and was married to Hatshepsut, princess of the royal blood. As luck would have it, Thutmose II and Hatshepsut had only daughters, and the problem of a legitimate successor arose yet again. Thutmose II died in 1505 B.C., perhaps of chagrin over the plethora of princesses, and yet another illegitimate son became Thutmose III. But the new pharaoh was a mere boy, and so Queen Hatshepsut, his step-mother, acted as regent, consolidating all power in her own hands. She became used to wielding the royal crook and scourge, symbols of the pharaoh's authority, and also dressed and acted as though she were the pharaoh—even wearing the traditional stylized beard. Her rule as a man lasted 22 years before her death allowed Thutmose III to take his rightful place. Thutmose then had a brilliant reign lasting until 1450 B.C.

The **Temple of Hatshepsut** is

unique in all Egypt, being built as a series of terraces on a grand scale, with stark colonnades blending in with the grooved mountainside which rises behind the temple. Hathor is the honoured goddess here, and murals showing the sacred cow are everywhere. The rooms behind the colonnade on the second terrace hold well-preserved paintings. The ceiling in the Chapel of Hathor at the southwestern (left) end of the terrace is as starry and blue as any night-time Egyptian sky, and the yellow hues are as bright as reflected sunlight.

On your way to the renowned Valley of the Kings, stop at **Gurnah** for a look at the funerary temple of Seti I (19th Dynasty), father of Ramesis II. Little is left of the temple's first two pylons and courts, but the hypostyle hall is filled with scenes showing Seti I and his ubiquitous son Ramesis II making offerings to Thebes' great god Amon.

Hieroglyphs

By the time Upper and lower Egypt were united in 3000 B.C., ancient Egyptians had an answer to their need for an alphabet: 24 simple-to-use pictorial letters. But temple priests and scribes soon turned this easy answer into a complex problem when they filled the hieroglyphic alphabet with some 700 signs and arcane symbols which only they could understand. The use of hieroglyphs died out at the end of the 4th century A.D., though the ancient Egyptian language continued to be spoken by Copts.

The art of reading hieroglyphic inscriptions remained a mystery for centuries until Napoleon's soldiers found the three-language Rosetta Stone in 1799. With the help of the Stone, Jean-François Champollion, a French scholar, cracked the hieroglyphic code and discovered that hieroglyphs can be written right-to-left, left-to-right, or up-and-down. You can easily tell which way, because the animals always stare toward the beginning of the sentence.

Kings and queens enclosed their names in "cartouches". Here are two famous royal monograms you may see in temples and tombs:

Cleopatra   Ptolemy

Valley of the Kings

The western bank of the Nile, closer to where the sun began its nightly course through the nether world, was always the preferred place for tombs. Pharaohs of the 18th, 19th and 20th Dynasties chose this forbidding rock valley for their eternal resting-place. Undisturbed by the annual rising of the Nile waters and hidden away in rock-hewn sepulchres with secret, sealed entrances, they were well fitted out for their underworld journey. Furnishings and costumes, mummiform statues or carved figures to act as servants and concubines, as well as food and a variety of drinks were all carefully included in each tomb. The royal voyagers even had a detailed guidebook to the dangers of the celestial journey—a copy of the Book of the Dead was standard tomb equipment. At the end of the trip they would meet the divine Osiris who would enlist the aid of Anubis and Thoth, gods of funeral rights and of wisdom, in judging the new arrivals: a pharaoh's heart would be weighed in a balance against a

Rock-hewn tombs concealed many treasures. Right: King Tut lived—and died—amid golden splendour.

feather, and if it was not heavy with sin, the pharaoh would be admitted to a pleasant life in the land of Osiris. In the Kingdom of Egypt which he had just left, he would take on an aura of deity like a lesser Osiris, and his family and loyal subjects would worship him in his funerary temple.

A king began work on his elaborate tomb and funeral equipment as soon as he came to power. Despite this admirable lack of procrastination, many monarchs had the misfortune to die before all was ready. They were immediately sealed up in their imperfect tombs as all the country's best artisans and craftsmen marched off to begin work on the new king's tomb. Though tombs might be guarded for centuries, and the hidden entrances lost to living memory, the ingenuity of grave-robbers increased along with the richness of the spoils. In the thousands of years since the New Kingdom, thieves suc-

ceeded in finding and breaking into every tomb—except one.

As you walk up the crunching gravel path to the Rest-House, the **Tomb of Tutankhamon,** No. 62, will be right before you. Though the tomb is very modest—the king died unexpectedly and was buried in a hurry—it is the only pharaonic tomb ever discovered intact. The dazzling wealth of this single lesser king makes it almost impossible to imagine the total extent of riches once secreted in this forbidding valley.

Sacred apes glower from the walls of Tutankhamon's small, simple tomb, and four shapely maidens are carved into his sarcophagus to protect him. The gilded mummy-case within the sarcophagus contains the king's mortal remains. The solid-gold inner coffin has been removed to the Egyptian Museum in Cairo, along with the other treasures from the tomb. (See p. 40.)

Perhaps the most splendid tomb in the Valley of the Kings is the **Tomb of Seti I,** No. 17, south of the Rest-House. The murals in the descending rooms and corridors are still of striking beauty and freshness though they're over 3,000 years old. The lowest room once held the king's massive alabaster sarcophagus: it is now in the Soane Museum in London. The semi-cylindrical vault over the sarcophagus-spot is painted as a blue sky with gods, goddesses and animals among the starry constellations. Seti's great tomb was unfinished when he died, as you can see from the wall paintings and excavation work in the lowest chambers.

Back down the path from Seti's tomb, keep to the left to reach the **Tomb of Ramesis III,** No. 11. A fine yellow-gold solar disc over the doorway leads to a corridor with many small side-chambers bearing interesting and unusual illustrations of daily crafts and labours. In one picture, two harpists sing the praises of Ramesis III before the gods, adding music to this frenzy of terrestrial and celestial activity.

The **Tomb of Horemheb,** No. 57, is only a few steps west of No. 11. The paintings here are particularly unusual, done on a dark background to achieve a heightened dramatic effect. In the last room, the artists had hardly even completed the preliminary sketches in red, when Horemheb was ready to start his trip to the land of Osiris.

Complicated rites and ceremonies awaited pharaoh in the Next World.

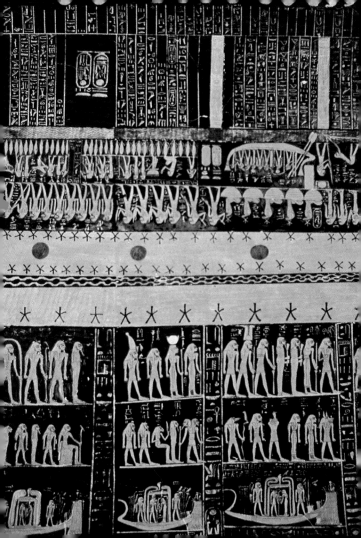

Follow the western (right-hand) path from Horemheb's tomb to get to No. 35, the **Tomb of Amenophis II,** which is at the end of it. The paintings in the tomb are plain and of subdued colour, but very finely done. The king's richly decorated sandstone sarcophagus is still in place.

You must do some climbing and scrambling to get to the **Tomb of Thutmose III,** No. 34. It is the farthest south from the Rest-House, along a narrow path and up a steel stairway, then down another stairway and through a tiny entrance. Its decoration is very plain, with colour used quite sparingly, though the result is attractive.

Sixty-two royal tombs have been uncovered so far in the Valley of the Kings, of which thirteen are usually open to the public. Repair and preservation work continues, and you should not be surprised if one or more tombs are closed temporarily.

After the hot and dusty tramp around the tombs, the cool, breezy terrace of the Rest-House beckons. Prices for coffee, tea or cold drinks are higher than need be, but after the thrill of exploring the valley's artistic riches, a few minutes' relaxation are essential to absorb the wealth of impressions.

Living right next to things incredibly ancient never loses its thrill, as at Edfu Temple, above.

From Luxor to Aswan

On the way up-river, at **Esna**, 60 kilometres south of Luxor, you'll find the **temple** dedicated to Khnum, the god who created men and animals by moulding them from Nile clay. Centuries of daily life on this spot have raised the level of the ground so that the temple now lies well below street level. Because the temple was filled with sand and rubble for centuries, it was protected to a certain extent. Excavations revealed the hypostyle hall of a temple first built in the 18th Dynasty, and completely reconstructed in the time of the Ptolemies and of the Romans, when Egyptian decorative art was in deep decline.

Farther along the river, midway between Luxor and Aswan, the large town of **Edfu** holds Egypt's best-preserved temple. Dedicated to Horus, the multiform god of the sun and planets, the hawk (symbol of the god) is prominent in its decoration. One reason the temple is so well preserved is that it was finished very late, only a few decades before Antony and Cleopatra held sway over Egypt. Take a horse-drawn carriage from the Nile's bank, and in five minutes it will bring you, bones still rattling, to the temple grounds.

The **Temple of Horus** has a huge pylon, almost as big as Karnak's. Thirty-eight columns surround the court, and a very fine granite statue of Horus stands guard over the entry to the first hypostyle hall. Every available surface is carved with hieroglyphs describing offerings to the god. In the very centre of the holy of holies is a great block of granite hollowed out as a sanctuary, with another block standing in front of it to bear the sacred barque. A modern copy of the barque itself is on view in the room directly behind the god's sanctuary. Other small chambers, lit only by tiny windows in the stone, preserve the sombre gloom. This is rarely seen in other temples which are often roofless, letting in the brilliant sunlight.

A modest restaurant near the entrance to the temple grounds provides refreshments and a cool place to sit. The parade of shoeshine boys, souvenir vendors and bright-eyed children passing by your table will provide more amusement than you'll ever need.

Continuing along the Nile, your first view of the temple at Kom Ombo will fill you with excitement. It stands right on the Nile's eastern bank, looking just like a Nile-side temple should look. Unique in all Egypt, **Kom Ombo Temple** is shared equally by two gods: Sobek, the crocodile god of Nile fertility, and Haroeris, the great winged solar disc. The first temple rose during the time of the 18th Dynasty, but virtually all you see was built much later under the Ptolemies in the three centuries before the birth of Christ.

Everything here is in pairs: double doorways lead into the great court and through the two hypostyle halls to a double sanctuary. To make the temple come alive, try to imagine the doorways fitted with their massive wooden doors, and the walls, columns and arches glowing with rich colours in the semi-darkness of the roofed interior.

To the right of the temple entrance is a small chapel dedicated to Hathor, now containing

Breathtaking immensity of Kom Ombo, temple shared by two gods.

an unusual legacy: some mummified crocodiles sacred to Sobek. North of the temple court a stone staircase descends in a spiral to the local Nilometre at the bottom of a circular well.

Sleepy Nubian town gets visitors. Rescued column hardly shows cuts.

Aswan

The town of Aswan (pop. 200,000) awakened in the 1960s to a flood of foreign engineers who had come to plan construction of an immense dam across the Nile. The Aswan High Dam (Sad el-Aali) was built by teams of engineers from the Soviet Union who directed a crew of

35,000 Egyptians in the work. The electricity and flood control facilities that it provided brought profound changes to the economy and agriculture of the country. While not all of the results of its construction had been foreseen, as ecological experts are now beginning to fear, most agree that the benefits of the project outweigh the disadvantages. When the enormous dam was completed in 1972, the town changed character completely.

Once a smaller version of Luxor, a town of farmers, holiday-makers and archaeologists, Aswan became an industrial centre with factories for iron

and steel, fertilizer chemicals, and sugar. Today, despite the changes all around it, the centre of town retains the same pleasant quality that once made it a favoured wintering spot for the late Aga Khan and other wealthy visitors. White-sailed feluccas, like great one-winged water birds, slip rapidly up and down the Nile, dodging among the islands. Horse carts stand at the entrances of hotels, waiting for tourists to climb in for a clip-clop ride among the eucalyptus, citrus and palm trees. The gold and grey of the desert hills is best at dawn, when the twitter of birds and braying of donkeys signal the beginning of yet another perfectly sunny day.

While you're here, go by taxi to the **High Dam** (about 10 kilometres from town). In the lotus-shaped monument to Soviet-Egyptian cooperation you can take a lift to the top for a fine view of the dam and Lake Nasser. The lake extends over 500 kilometres south, past the Egyptian frontier and into the Sudan.

Industry of a different sort brought wealth to Aswan in pharaonic times. The beautiful red granite from which obelisks were cut is native to the town, and a few minutes' ride by taxi from the centre will bring you to the quarries. A mammoth **unfinished obelisk,** fractured during cutting and abandoned, shows how these magnificent monuments were painstakingly hewn by hand and polished to a glassy smoothness.

Aswan is a good place to hire a felucca for a tour of the islands and the western bank of the Nile. **Elephantine Island,** the largest, holds the ruined Temple of Khnum, the work of many pharaohs down to the Ptolemies and even the Romans. The Aswan Museum, housed in an early-20th-century villa, is right next to the ruins. The set of stairs cut in the rock below the villa descends to Aswan's Nilometre, where you'll see the elegant marble water-level markers still in place. **Kitchener's Island** (or Island of Flowers) was a gift to the influential Consul-General of Great Britain in Egypt, and now serves as a botanical garden. It's one of Aswan's most pleasant places for a stroll. At the island's southern tip is a duck research station—just follow the sound of the quacky cacaphony. As you might imagine, this is a favourite destination for Aswan's children.

On the hills above the western bank of the Nile stands the **Mausoleum of the Aga Khan,** whose full title was Sultan Muhammad Shah Al-Huseini,

Aga Khan III, 48th Imam of the Shia Imami Ismailis, which is a Moslem sect whose adherents live chiefly in Iran and Pakistan. The Aga Khan (1877–1957) built a villa in Aswan just below the mausoleum, fell in love with the spot, and decided to stay forever. From the mausoleum, a path winds across the desert sand to the ruined 7th-century **Monastery of St. Simeon.**

North along the Nile's west bank lies a typical Nubian village where life moves at an easy pace much as it did in centuries past. Ducks, donkeys and goats amble in the streets, young girls fetch buckets of water from a Nile canal, and groups of boys devote themselves to a hectic game of football. Remember that if you plan to photograph or film villagers, you must always ask their permission in advance.

Above the village, tombs of local potentates known as the Lords of Elephantine Island are carved in the rock. Some interesting traces of decoration survive, as do pigeons and bats in disconcerting abundance. A few tombs contain stone blocks on which offerings were sacrificed, and one tomb, the 12th Dynasty tomb of Sarambot I (or Sirenput), is complete with the mummy of Mrs. Sarambot who welcomes you in, "staring" with eyeless sockets in the shadowy light. With a few actors and a camera crew, these tombs would yield a very convincing horror film in no time at all. But they are among the oldest in Egypt, and a visit to the hillside ledge affords a fine view of Aswan and the Nile.

Aswan has its share of great pharaonic temples. When many were threatened by the rising waters of Lake Nasser during construction of the High Dam, the most important ones were moved to higher ground.

The famous **Temples of Philae** are a case in point. Before the first Aswan Dam was built, around 1900, the temples formed on Philae Island one of Egypt's most impressive sights; they were then partially submerged until the High Dam operations threatened them with total disappearance. In a vast international rescue effort coordinated by UNESCO, they were reassembled in all their glory on the island of Agilkia, some 300 yards to the north.

The **Great Temple of Isis** flourished at about the time of Christ, and is the largest and most distinctive of the island temples. Unfortunately, the secret stairway inside the great pylon can no longer be viewed—or climbed.

Another taxi-ride to a different dock, and then a rental boat, will get you to **temples** from Kalabsha, which were once located on the banks of the Nile some 50 kilometres to the south. The temples were moved here closer to Aswan and to its appreciative tourists with the financial help of the Federal Republic of Germany. Largest is the **Temple of Mandoulis,** a classic Egyptian temple built in Roman times. To the left of the entrance to Mandoulis is the pretty little **Temple of Kertassi,** with capitals bearing the half-human, half-bovine face of Hathor. Behind the Temple of Mandoulis is **Beit El-Wali,** moved with American aid from its former site. The temple's murals show the military campaigns of Ramesis II in wars against various unattractive and easily defeated foreign enemies.

✝ Abu Simbel

Of the many thrills which await visitors to Egypt, from that first glimpse of the pyramids to a quiet moment in Karnak's great hypostyle hall, few are more moving than when one stands face-to-face with the four colossal statues of Ramesis II at Abu Simbel. If possible, stay overnight at the small hotel here and rise early to see the sun illuminate the temple façade and penetrate to the depths of its inner sanctum.

Here at the limits of Upper Egypt, Ramesis II built his temple in honour of Harmakhis (Guardian of the Gates to the Nether World), Amon-Ra (Solar God), Ptah (God of Creativity), and in honour of himself, Ramesis II. The **four colossal figures,** 60 feet high and directly facing the rising sun, are all of pharaoh himself, with his queen and daughters at his feet. Above the entryway is the high-relief figure of Amon-Ra. A row of baboons, symbols of wisdom, sit hunched along the upper border of the tall façade. More tremendous statues surround you as you enter the **temple,** these being of Ramesis II in the guise of Osiris. Bas-reliefs on all sides tell of the monarch's generous offerings to the gods, of his triumphant military campaigns, and his merciless treatment of captives. In the very depths of the temple, Ramesis II sits in state with the gods to whom the construction is dedicated. The perfection of Ramesis' accomplishment is echoed in the restoration work planned by a Swedish firm and carried out in 1968–72 by UNESCO. A doorway to the right of the façade leads to the interior of the artificial moun-

For prolific builder Ramesis II, happiness was reproduction—of himself.

tain made to receive the temple. Charts and diagrams tell the story (in English) of the temple's move from a spot now inundated by Lake Nasser to its new, air-conditioned man-made site.

The caretaker, bearing the giant *ankh* (life symbol) which is the temple key, will let you into the smaller **Temple of Hathor.** Four of the statues on the façade are of Ramesis II, while the other two show his queen, Nefertari, dressed as the goddess Hathor. Interior decoration is heavily in favour of the feminine side of the Egyptian pantheon although, predictably, Ramesis II is here as well. The benevolent cow in the depths of the temple is Hathor in her animal guise.

Photographers should visit Abu Simbel as early as possible, for the statues throw heavy shadows as the day wears on. Everyone who arrives at this spellbinding place, over 600 miles from the noise and bustle of Cairo, will want to take a few peaceful moments to gaze at Lake Nasser, a tranquil sea in the midst of the timeless desert. **83**

What to Do

Shopping

Cairo's **Khan el-Khalili** is world-famous for its wealth of things to buy. Antique or modern, simple or elegant, some handicraft item is bound to draw your eye. You'll need to haggle, but will be rewarded for your efforts by a truly remarkable change in price. Don't take a guide or interpreter when you go shopping as it is standard practice for him to get a kickback on every purchase. Sometimes, a detour to the workshop in a back street or roof-top room will give you the chance to buy at a reduced price.

Here are some of Egypt's best buys, available in Khan el-Khalili and in tourist shops and markets in other cities, too:

Alabaster. The word itself is said to derive from the name of an Egyptian town. Shops sell statuettes, cigarette boxes, flower vases and similar items made from it. The stone comes from the Nile Valley and is worked, among other places, in Luxor.

Antiquities. Although it was once permissible for licensed dealers to sell genuine antique pieces of jewellery and artefacts from pharaonic times, this trade is no longer legal.

If you are caught at the airport transporting antiquities, the penalties are stiff. Fakes abound, however, and may make quaint souvenirs—as long as they don't cost too much.

Copper and Brass. The tinkling of coppersmith's hammers is a familiar sound in Khan

el-Khalili. The best trays, Turkish coffee sets, samovars and other items are generally the older ones, but new copper and brass pieces are often cheaper, and still attractive and useful. It takes about a day and a half to chisel the arabesques into a small copper serving tray.

Cotton goods. Egyptian cotton's long fibres and smooth finish make it among the highest grades in the world. Mohammed Ali built the wealth of his dynasty on cotton. Many shirt-makers' shops

Gimcracks, antiquities, beguiling folk-arts: the choice is yours.

unpolished cotton will be cheaper than the more chic polished cloth.

Jewellery. Gold and silver jewellery is often sold by weight with only a small mark-up for the exquisite detailed workmanship. Take your pick from pharaonic styles inspired by King Tutankhamon's treasure, arabesques, or modern pieces. Precious and semi-precious stones are also sold by weight at attractive prices, whether set in a piece of jewellery or not. Generally speaking, it's best to shop around before buying.

Leather Goods. Handbags, satchels and shoulder bags are all good buys if you bargain well, but it's important to inspect each piece very carefully for flaws and careless workmanship. Some shops sell camel saddles. They're hard to find outside Egypt, but before buying you should ask yourself: does my camel really need a new one yet?

Tapestries. The eye-catching designs worked in cloth by the children of El-Harraniye (a village between Giza and Saqqara) can brighten any wall or liven any table-top. They come in different sizes, although colours and motifs will probably be your criteria of choice. The true Harraniye tapestries tend to be rather expensive, and

throughout Egypt will stitch up shirts to your order in a few days, or you can choose from the ready-made ones. *Gallabiyas,* the long and loose Egyptian outer garments, are comfortable and attractive, and are made for both men and women. Be sure to look at several sizes and qualities of cloth:

you may want to look at the less expensive copies and imitations (good and bad) which have come on the market.

Woodwork. Some of the most attractive woodwork in the world comes from Egypt. Foremost is *mashrabiyya,* the intricate screens of lathe-turned wooden lattice which covered Egyptian windows in the old days, shielding women from the curious stares of strange men. Screens, room-dividers and tray-stands are

Left, careful work makes each piece a unique treasure. Below, cloth for sale in Khan el-Khalili.

sold at reasonable prices, but you ought to consider the problems of transportation before you buy. An alternative choice, easily jammed into a suitcase, is a small box of cedar or sandalwood inlaid with bits of ivory, mother-of-pearl and ebony. Each tiny piece of inlay is glued in by hand, set in place with a pair of tweezers. If you have space in your luggage, consider one of the larger boxes or perhaps an inlaid chessboard or small table.

Folklore and Festivals

Festival time in Egypt finds everyone outdoors, following processions in the streets, strolling along the Nile, or filling the parks and gardens. Vendors sell snacks and refreshing drinks, and the crowds eagerly pay court to itinerant performers. Wrestlers, dancers and singers all put on open-air shows, happily collecting coins at the end of the performance.

A favourite diversion is the

mock-battle called El-Tahtib: two men, armed with stout reed staffs, face each other and walk in a circle while swinging the staffs above their heads. It looks like a courtly dance, but each combatant is tingling with alertness, waiting for the opportunity to take a swing at his opponent. A split-second of inattention by one player, and the heavy staff of the other speeds down, but there's time to parry, and the two weapons meet with a resounding thwack. With equally-matched players. El-Tahtib becomes a graceful ceremony of smooth movements and mutual respect. But let a wily old master take on a young and inexperienced hot-blood, and the blows fall thick and fast. Strength and agility are less important than experience and alertness, and the old man

Lively African rhythms punctuate Nubian songs. In El-Tahtib, one inattentive moment spells defeat.

always ends up teaching the novice a few fine tricks.

In Upper Egypt, Nubian folklore and music is very different from the Arabic folklore of Cairo and the delta. Nubians have their own languages (though most speak Arabic as well), and traditional Nubian music sounds surprisingly Far Eastern in its tonalities and rhythms.

All Egyptians are united in the celebration of major Islamic and traditional festivals. The National Spring Festival, Sham en-Nessim, comes on the Monday following Coptic Easter. It's an excuse for everyone to get outdoors or into boats on the Nile in order to obey an old legend. "He who sniffs the first spring zephyr", so it goes, "will have good health all year". Another major holiday is Mulid en-Nabi, the Prophet's Birthday, when a mammoth procession winds through Cairo's streets, imitated by smaller ones in other cities.

Ramadan is a period of 30 days in the ninth month of the Moslem lunar calendar. During this time, all good Moslems observe strict fasting between the hours of sunrise and sunset. The rules are strict: no food or drink, no smoking or even licking a stamp beginning at first light. Working hours are also reduced. The fast is broken at sunset, and special dishes fill the feast tables for the early evening breakfast meal of *iftar*. Children, pregnant women, travellers and the infirm are exempted from the fast, and everyone else takes advantage of shorter working hours. Tourist hotels and restaurants keep normal, year-round hours for the convenience of non-Moslem visitors though many stop serving alcoholic drinks. At the end of the holy month comes Ramadan Bairam *(Eid el-Fitr)*, a three-day celebration marked by gifts of greeting-cards, and visits among friends.

Perhaps the most sacred of Moslem festivals, Qurban Bairam *(Eid el-Adha)* comes in the middle of the month of Zu'l-Hegga, when many Moslems make the *hajj*, or pilgrimage, to Mecca. The four-day feast commemorates the biblical near-sacrifice by Abraham of his son, and Moslem families relive the moment by sacrificing a ram. After the ritual slaughter according to Koranic law, the meat is cooked and a feast is prepared for family and friends, with a generous portion going to the poor.

August used to be a time of elaborate festivals in Cairo. As the waters of the Nile rose in the annual flood, Nilometres all along the river would be checked and rechecked, and the readings sent off to Cairo by messenger. When the water level reached a certain point, all the canals would be unblocked and the precious water would surge deep into the fields carrying valuable silt to replenish the soil. Now that the Aswan High Dam controls the Nile's flow at an even level all year round, the August festivities have only the faintest echo of their former gaiety and importance.

The Cairo Film Festival was first organized in 1977 and proved a great success. Many countries bring their award-winning films to be shown at some of the best hotels at specific times during one week. The festival is generally held in November.

Sports and Recreation

Cairo and Alexandria have many sporting clubs once patronized only by wealthy foreigners and Egyptian nobility. Today they're much more democratic, and tourists are invited to use the facilities as temporary or short-term members. In the heart of Cairo on the island of Gezira are dozens of tennis courts a racetrack, a golf course, squash and handball courts, several swimming pools and every other imaginable sports facility. Due to sheer weight of numbers, they are often highly exclusive clubs, with strict admittance requirements and a hefty annual membership fee. Clubs which take on temporary members are: Cairo Yacht Club, Heliopolis Sporting Club, Maadi Sporting Club, Maadi Yacht Club, Mena Golf Club and the Shooting Club.

Water Sports. As long as you don't swim in the Nile, you can enjoy a lot of water fun during your stay in Egypt. Besides the miles of beaches in Alexandria and along the Mediterranean coast, swimming amenities are offered by almost every large hotel and are open to outsiders on payment of a sizeable annual fee.

Hurghada on the Egyptian Red Sea coast offers hotel and beach facilities, and the best conditions in the country for scuba diving and snorkelling. Flights from Cairo and shared taxis or bus from Luxor are the best way to reach Hurghada.

The return of the Sinai Peninsula to Egypt under the peace treaty with Israel opened up some glorious holiday opportunities for visitors. Nuwaiba and Dahab on the Gulf **91** of Aqaba and Sharm al-Sheikh on the Red Sea are three well-known resorts of international standard, proposing all manner of water sports as well as superb beaches for simply soaking up the sun.

Riding. Whether your preference is sunlight or moonlight, you can rent a mount for an hour or a day, with a guide or without. Rates are very reasonable, though you may have to do some haggling. Most exciting of all trails is the one which takes you from the stables at the pyramids of Giza along the edge of the desert to the pyramids at Abusir and Saqqara.

Nightlife

Sound-and-light Shows

The grandeur of the pyramids is magnified at night when powerful floodlights bathe the ancient stones with rich colour. A stirring commentary enhanced with symphonic music comes from hidden loudspeakers. Sound-and-light shows at the pyramids are given in English on Monday, Wednesday, Thursday, Friday and Saturday nights. Check performance times, as these vary with the time of the year. You can take a taxi to the pyramids and pay the entry fee yourself, or you can join an all-inclusive bus tour.

A show is held at the Great Temple of Amon at Karnak. After strolling through the temple, spectators sit in banks of seats behind the Sacred Lake.

One important thing to keep in mind for a sound-and-light show: no one ever seems to dress warmly enough, despite warnings of the evening's chill.

Cinemas

Look in the local English-language newspapers for current film showings. Something is always playing in English or at least with English subtitles. In Egypt's cinemas everyone has a reserved seat.

Buy your tickets an hour or more in advance (a particularly good idea on Thursday, Friday or Saturday night).

Recreational possiblities are plentiful even in central Cairo. **93**

Clubs

Clubs in the large hotels offer nightly variety shows, with Western song-and-dance reviews followed by fiery Egyptian music. When your blood is racing, on comes the belly-dancer, and the music builds to fever-pitch as she performs her sinuous gyrations and muscular impossibilities. Music for dancing follows. Though exciting and entertaining, hotel shows are not risqué, and can be enjoyed even by those who might take offence at the Folies Bergère.

Many hotel clubs and discotheques require membership or expensive door charges to enter. Men without escorts might not be allowed in at some of them. Dance music is from the latest records, but a belly-dancer and oriental band often help to improve the entertainment.

The Pyramids Road is lined with flashy nightspots, mostly for lone men with money to burn. It's generally better for couples to find the current "in" spot in the city centre.

Dramatic sound-and-light shows shed new light on old monuments.

Opera House

The Opera House was an official gift from the Japanese government in 1988. The complex, which also houses several art galleries, is a must when visiting Cairo. Operas, with foreign and Egyptian performances, are staged from October to May. Check, in case semi-formal or formal dress is required.

Casinos

Foreigners are the only ones allowed into Egypt's gambling houses, so bring along your passport. Only foreign currency may be used at the tables. Most luxury hotels have casinos. If you see "Casino" on a sign by a Nile-side restaurant, don't be fooled. In the Middle East, a casino is a waterside establishment which can be anything from a snack bar to a restaurant with floor show but there will *definitely* not be any gambling.

National Circus

Egypt's National Circus was started with the help of Soviet circus masters some time ago. The clowns, acrobats and animals perform in Cairo's Agouza quarter during most of the year, moving to Alexandria for the hot months of July and August.

Dining

In a country with such a long history, it's intriguing to think that as a modern-day visitor to Egypt you might be eating the same as the pharaohs did. Certainly many things are unchanged. Mediterranean and Red Sea fish are served, and the Nile valley and the delta yield sheep, cattle, game, pigeons and ducks, grain and vegetables just as they appear in the old wall paintings. But more recent history has also had a culinary impact on Egyptian food. Italian, Turkish, French and English influences are all to be found in Egyptian cookery. Present-day internationalism provides an additional touch as well: from *chow mein* to *wienerschnitzel*, from Wimpy Bars to Colonel Sanders—it's all yours in Cairo.

Egyptians dine lightly at breakfast. In your hotel, the normal continental breakfast of coffee or tea, toast and rolls, butter and jam may be supplemented with salty white or pale yellow cheese, and fresh fruit juice.

Lunch is the main meal of the day, though many hotels cater to foreign habits and serve the big dinner in the evening. One o'clock until three or four in the afternoon is the usual lunch-break.

Dinner in Egyptian homes is traditionally served quite late, perhaps not until 10 p.m. or even later. During Ramadan all these hours, and many of the foods served, change completely.

Egyptian Cuisine

Your hotel is liable to serve more European dishes than Egyptian ones, but you should not miss any chance to savour the local fare. For an interesting sampling, many restaurants offer *mezzeh*—a selection of local salads, cheese, vine leaves and, sometimes, meat. A fun first course for a group of friends, *mezzeh* can even be a light meal in itself.

Or start off with *molokhia,* a soup of the green leafy vegetable cooked in broth with garlic, pepper and coriander, usually eaten with rice. Most Egyptians get along well on *fool,* a thick and savoury stew of beans flavoured with tomatoes and spices. It's delicious and is commonly served with oil and the juice of a lime or with *taamia,* a paste made of the same beans plus other vegetables, mixed with parsley and spices and deep-fried. *Makhallal (turshi)* spicy pickled vegetables, show up frequently on Egyptian tables.

Bread is the flat Middle Eastern type, especially well-suited for scooping up mouthfuls of *leben zabadi* (yogurt), or *tahina* (sesame seed puree), or its variation *baba ganoug* (*tahina* with puree of baked aubergine/eggplant, lemon and garlic).

Some restaurants specialize in *kebab,* succulent chunks of lamb or mutton marinated in spices and grilled over charcoal on a spit. A variation is *kofta,* minced or ground lamb spiced and wrapped around a flat skewer to be grilled the same way, over charcoal, then served on a bed of fresh parsley or coriander leaf.

Fish from the Mediterranean or Lake Nasser is pan- or deep-fried, sometimes with an unexpected pinch of cumin added during cooking. Large Alexandrian shrimp are a delicacy, and are grilled on a skewer over a fragrant charcoal brazier.

Egyptians love to dine on pigeons, the birds being split and grilled or stuffed, served on a bed of rice.

Salads are served before and during the main course. Boiled cold beetroot is popular in season, and you will find it difficult to stop eating the excellent ripe sliced tomatoes and cucumbers with a dash of lemon juice or vinegar. Green salads may contain a tart, almost peppery green leaf called *gargir* mixed with the lettuce. Once you've tasted it, chances are you'll want to have it again.

Egyptian cheese is a disappointment, as even the best comes heavily salted. This may be good for water retention in a desert climate, but it's no treat for an unaccustomed palate. Processed cheese wrapped in foil is widely available.

For dessert, you can never go wrong with fresh fruit from the Delta such as bananas, oranges, figs or guavas. A basket of fruit will contain fresh dates, which are different from the dried, sweet dates you may have had elsewhere. Whenever you see it on the menu, order *ommu-'ali,* a baked dessert of rice, milk, raisins and coconut. It tastes delicious when made badly, and is heavenly when made well. Cakes and pastries are also easy to find, but must take

second place to fresh fruit or *ommu-'ali*.

Tourist hotels often neglect to serve many delicious Egyptian desserts, but should you see them offered, you must try *baklawa*, a many layered pastry stuffed with nuts and honey; an alternative is *'atayeef,* a deep-fried pastry with either sweet or cheese filling, served principally during Ramadan. *Mahallabiyah* is a fairly bland pudding of rice and milk garnished with nuts.

European Cuisine

Traditionally in Egyptian tourist hotels, local cuisine is banished from the menu almost entirely and its place taken by "international" cuisine, with only the best hotels employing foreign-born chefs. Depending on a number of factors, therefore, this cuisine can be bland, merely undistinguished or, occasionally, sublime. If you crave something more than your hotel offers, ask your concierge about the

restaurants' in the residential areas of Zamalek and Giza, then take a taxi off on an adventure. These restaurants are relatively inexpensive and with a little luck you won't be disappointed.

Beverages

Moslems are forbidden to drink alcohol. Though many Egyptians enjoy a glass of beer, the religious prohibition of alcohol means that soft drinks are very popular, and found everywhere. Many popular, western-style soft drinks are bottled under licence in Egypt, including low-calorie versions. You may find them less fizzy and sweeter than you're used to. Fruit juices are almost always available and sometimes they will be fresh-squeezed. Be sure to try the Egyptian speciality called *karkadeh,* a deep-red infusion of hibiscus petals with an agreeable flavour, served slightly sweetened. It's delicious cold at breakfast-time, but can be a bracing pick-me-up served hot as well. Hotels and restaurants in Upper Egypt, where the plant grows, serve it frequently. Sug-

After the pyramids, what next? A peaceful Nile-side café or a cool drink in a shady bazaar—perfect!

ar-cane juice is also cheap and flavourful.

Egyptian vineyards in the Delta have been cultivated for centuries. All hotel restaurants serve wine, though the selection may be limited, and service suspended on Moslem religious holidays. The price for a bottle of wine in a hotel restaurant will **99** be about three times the shop price. Buy a bottle and have the steward mark it with your room number so that if you don't finish it at one meal you can enjoy it at the next. Of the reds, *Omar Khayyam* and *Chateau* (or *Kasr*) *Gianaclis* are soft, fairly dry, and have a good deal of tannin. *Pharaons* is less tasty and slightly more dry. White wines, often better than the red, but invariably served too warm, are *Nefertiti, Cleopatra,* and *Gianaclis Villages.* If you prefer rosé, ask for *Rubis d'Egypte* and insist that it be ice-cold. Local wine is definitely an acquired taste, but imported table wine, when available, can more than double the price of your meal.

Several imported brands of beer are served in better hotels and restaurants, always relatively expensive. Local beer, a light lager called *Stella,* comes in large bottles which easily serve two people. It's quite drinkable, though *Stella Export,* in smaller bottles at a higher price, is preferred by some.

Local spirits are made from grapes or dates. *Zibib,* the Egyptian version of aniseed-flavoured *arak* (like *ouzo* or *pastis*), may be made from either grape brandy or date brandy. Many visitors find the grape variety preferable. Locally made vodka is good. Imported spirits take a prominent place in high-class hotel and restaurant bars.

Tea and Turkish Coffee

French or American-style coffee served in Egypt is not often brewed with care, and you may prefer the instant variety. Tea *(shay)* is popular with Egyptians and tourists alike. As a refresher served in an Arabic coffee house, it will come with sprigs of mint. Stir a few into your glass: Egyptians swear it improves digestion and gives extra energy.

Turkish coffee is usually very good. It's served on the slightest pretext. An Egyptian host who didn't serve coffee to visitors—even on a five-minute visit to a shop, office or home —would be looked upon as a national disgrace. Most foreigners come to prefer Turkish coffee when it's brewed *mazbut* (with a middling amount of sugar). If it tastes too bitter order it *ziyada* (with lots of sugar). *Saadeh* is with no sugar at all. *Arrihah* means your tiny cup will come flavoured with just the slightest pinch of sugar. In practice, one is never quite sure exactly how the coffee will come, as one coffee-maker's *arrihah* is another's *mazbut*.

To Help You Order...

I would like a/an/some...   *orid*   ... اريد

beer	*bira*	بيرة	mineral	*mayya*	مياه معدنية
bread	*esh*	عيش (خبز)	water	*madaniyya*	
butter	*zibda*	زبدة	mustard	*mostarda*	مسترده (خردل)
cheese	*gibna*	جبنة	olive	*zayt*	زيت زيتون
coffee	*ahwa*	قهوة	oil	*zayton*	
eggs	*baed*	بيض	pepper	*filfil*	فلفل (بهار)
fish	*samak*	سمك	potatoes	*batatis*	بطاطس
fruit	*fakha*	فاكهة	salad	*salata*	صلطة
fruit-	*aseer-*	عصير فاكهة	salt	*malh*	ملح
juice	*fakha*		soup	*shorba*	شوربة
ice-cream	*gelati*	جلاس (بوظة)	sugar	*sokkar*	سكر
lemon	*laymon*	ليمون (حامض)	tea	*shay*	شاي
meat	*lahm*	لحم	vegetables	*khodar*	خضار
milk	*laban haleab*	لبن حليب	wine	*nibit*	نبيذ

...and Read the Menu

فراخ	*firakh*	chicken	زيتون	*zayton*	olives
حمام	*hamam*	pigeon	بصل	*basal*	onions
رنجة	*ringa*	herring	رز	*roz*	rice
سردين	*sardin*	sardines	طماطم	*tamatim*	tomatoes
بفتيك	*boftek*	beef steak	(بندورة)		
ريش (كستليتة)	*riyash*	lamb	بلح	*balah*	dates
ضاني	*dani*	chops	تين	*teen*	figs
روسبيف	*rosbif*	roast beef	بطيخ	*battikh*	water-
كستليتة بتلو (عجل)	*kostaleta bitello*	veal chops			melon
باذنجان	*bitingan*	aubergine (eggplant)	فستق	*fostok*	pistachio
			كيك	*kek*	cake
حمص	*hommos*	chick-peas	مكرونة شريط	*makarona shirit*	noodles
ثوم	*toam*	garlic	مسلوق	*maslook*	boiled
عدس	*ads*	lentils	مقلي	*makli*	fried
بامية	*bamia*	okra	مشوي	*mashwi*	grilled

101

BLUEPRINT for a Perfect Trip

How to Get There

Because of the complexity and variability of the many fares, you should ask the advice of an informed travel agent well before your departure.

BY AIR

Scheduled Flights

Scheduled service operates daily from London's Heathrow and Gatwick airports. Irish and provincial flights make the connection in London for the four-hour non-stop flight to Cairo.

Daily direct flights link New York and Cairo, with connecting service available from major cities in the United States and Canada.

Charter Flights and Package Tours

From the United Kingdom: There is a wide range of package tours to Egypt, the more expensive ones including a cruise on the Nile with accommodation, meals and sightseeing. Some charter flights and cheaper options are now available to Luxor, as well as to Cairo, but as conditions are constantly changing, check with your travel agent before you leave.

From North America: There are currently dozens of GITs (Group Inclusive Tours) available to Egypt for periods of 7 to 22 days, with Cairo as the starting point. Tour features include round-trip air transportation, hotel accommodation, some or all meals, transfers and porterage, sightseeing, the services of an English-speaking guide, taxes, and all service charges. Optional features include a Nile river cruise, lasting from 4 to 8 days, or an air tour to Abu Simbel.

On certain charter flights available from New York to Cairo, you may be able (with the help of a travel agent) to get a flight at a price that is considerably lower than the normal airfare.

BY LAND AND SEA

You can take the train, or drive your car, to Venice or Athens to catch the ship to Alexandria. Few of them are true car ferries (though most carry cars), so it's particularly important to check sailing schedules and prices with your travel agent before leaving home, as well as booking your passage at least two weeks in advance.

Some Mediterranean cruise-ships also call at Alexandria, giving passengers the opportunity for a quick trip to Cairo and the pyramids.

When to Go

October and November are the most comfortable months to visit Egypt. April and May are also cool and pleasant, but are more unpredictable. Mid-winter weather can be very nippy although the constant dryness of the air and almost total absence of rain (except in Alexandria and along the northern coast) give Egypt a perfectly healthy climate for the time of the year. The winter season is the most crowded with higher prices and heavily booked hotels.

As all the best hotels, Nile cruise boats, tour buses and trains are air-conditioned, a visit to Egypt in summer is possible if you plan your sightseeing for early or late in the day, and take precautions against excessive sun and dryness.

The chart below shows average monthly temperatures in Cairo and Alexandria:

		J	F	M	A	M	J	J	A	S	O	N	D
Cairo	C°	14	15	18	21	23	27	29	28	26	24	20	15
	F°	57	59	64	70	76	81	84	82	79	75	68	59
Alexandria	C°	14	15	16	19	22	24	26	27	25	23	20	16
	F°	57	59	61	66	72	75	79	81	77	76	68	61

Planning Your Budget

To give you an idea of what to expect, here's a list of average prices in Egyptian pounds (L.E.) and piastres (pt.) and US$. Bear in mind that inflation is high in Egypt and many basic prices are raised even further by widespread tipping.

Airport. Porter 50 pt. per bag. Hire of baggage trolley L.E. 1. Taxi to centre of Cairo L.E. 27, by limousine L.E. 18.

Boat services. Felucca (per hour for entire boat) L.E. 20–25 in Cairo, L.E. 20–25 in Aswan and Luxor. Nile bus 25 pt. to Old Cairo, 35 pt. to Nile Barrages.

Car hire (with unlimited mileage). *Fiat 128* $50–56 per day; *Fiat Nova Regata* (air conditioned) $72–83 per day; *Peugeot 505* (air conditioned estate) $86–117 per day. Add $1.25 personal insurance per day and 5% local tax.

Cigarettes. Egyptian filter brands L.E. 2 for 20, foreign brands L.E. 3.50.

Entertainment. Cinemas L.E. 2.50–5.50, discotheque L.E. 15–20, night-club (including dinner but not drinks) L.E. 40–60.

Guides. L.E. 10–15 per hour depending on language and place.

Hotels (double room with bath per night). Luxury class $ 120–160, first class $90–120, second class $40–75, third class $25–35. Add 12% service, 14% municipal tax. Breakfast L.E. 12–18 per day.

Meals and drinks. Continental breakfast L.E. 8–10, lunch/dinner in fairly good establishment L.E. 9–25, *fool* and *taamia* 50 pt.–L.E. 1.50, bottled soft drinks L.E. 1, coffee L.E. 1–1.50, local beer L.E. 4, imported beer (small can) L.E. 10, Egyptian wine (bottle) L.E. 12–14, cocktail L.E. 6–8, imported mineral water L.E. 2.50 per litre, local mineral water L.E. 1–1.50 per litre.

Museums. L.E. 5–10.

Nile cruises. 4 to 7 nights $344–800 per person double occupancy.

Transport. *Train* Cairo–Alexandria L.E. 12, to Luxor L.E. 28, to Aswan L.E. 35, special tourist train (overnight sleeper) Cairo to Luxor/Aswan, L.E. 216 per person including meals. *Air* Cairo–Luxor $75, Aswan $103, Abu Simbel $164, Hurghada $80, Sharm el Sheikh $85, Alexandria $42.

An A–Z Summary of Practical Information and Facts

> A star (*) following an entry indicates that relevant prices are to be found on page 105.
>
> Listed after some basic entries is the appropriate transcription of spoken Arabic, plus a number of phrases that should help you when seeking assistance.

A

AIRPORT*. Cairo airport has four terminals, three for international flights and one for domestic flights. The international terminals are equipped with café, restaurant, bar, banks (see MONEY MATTERS) and duty-free and souvenir shops. Have patience as you enter Egypt. If you have not yet changed money, you'll need to change a small amount for porters' tips and taxis. Visas are available for those who neglected to get them at home (see also ENTRY FORMALITIES AND CUSTOMS CONTROLS).

Customs inspections are usually perfunctory. You may be asked to open handbags and carry-on luggage by security officers. It's best to keep cameras out of sight, as photography is forbidden at airports.

For help with airport problems, contact the General Authority for the Promotion of Tourism desk in the arrivals terminal near the exit doors. They may be able to help you to find accommodation.

Make sure to book return tickets when you make initial arrangements for your holiday in your home country. Be certain to follow the regulations for reconfirmation of on-going or return reservations once you reach Egypt—flights are never sufficient to carry traffic demand, and you want to be sure of a seat.

On the day of your departure, allow *plenty* of time—two hours or more—to fight through Cairo's frenetic traffic so you'll be at the airport in time. The ride takes about 30 minutes if there is no traffic at all (as in the middle of the night). For details on airport transport and internal air routes, see TRANSPORT.

Airports at Alexandria, Luxor, Aswan and Abu Simbel are simple but adequate, with transport to the centre provided by both taxis and airport buses.

Taxi!	**taksi**
Where's the bus for…?	**fayn al otobís illi ráyih…**

BAKSHEESH. Tipping takes on a wider dimension in Egypt. Baksheesh, which once signified a foreigner's giving money to an Egyptian for no apparent reason, is virtually dead in its classical form, replaced by the custom of tipping for every service—no matter how small. Egyptians who have little contact with tourists rarely demand baksheesh, but those who work in tourist-related industries often depend on tips for their livelihood (which is helpful to bear in mind when the soliciting begins). In general, the larger the tip requested, the less urgent the need of the asker. You will have to obtain a large supply of coins and notes of 5, 10, 25 and 50 piastres to keep your trip running smoothly.

BICYCLE HIRE *(igár bisiklét)*. Bikes can be hired in Luxor on both sides of the Nile. Rates are low—if you bargain well—and the equipment is basic. Bicycling is a good way to see the various tombs and ruins of Luxor.

What's the charge per day?   **bekám fil yom**

BOAT SERVICES*. The romantic *feluccas* which ply the Nile waters are practical as well as picturesque. You can arrange to hire a boat and helmsman in any Nile town or village; many *felucca* owners are used to tourists and often anticipate just where you'll want to go. It's best to save your *felucca* cruise for Luxor or Aswan as rates in Cairo tend to be high; if you want to see Cairo by *felucca*, find others to share the cost with you. Check at the dock near the Hotel Méridien in Cairo or the yacht club in Maadi to make arrangements; in Luxor or Aswan, ask any boatman on the river (or, rather, they'll ask you), and be sure that the price, length of cruise and ports of call are well understood before you weigh anchor. The Tourism Office has an official boat-rental price list, which may or may not be honoured by your boatman; it can serve as a useful guide, however.

The Nile Bus motorized ferry plies between Old Cairo (south) and the Television Building in the north. The trip takes about 20–30 minutes and is well worth it.

One of the most exciting things to do in Egypt is to take an excursion of several days on a Nile cruise boat (see NILE CRUISES).

CAMPING *(mo'askar)*. Though camping is in its infancy in Egypt, several established campsites do exist in the Nile Valley, on the Mediterranean coast and Red Sea. Ask at the tourist office for further details.

C You can also camp on beaches, or in other open areas—provided you first obtain the permission of the local authorities. This is essential, since some Red Sea beaches are mined, while others are patrolled by military personnel who have been known to shoot after dark.

Can we camp here?   **múmkin mo'askar héna**

CAR HIRE*. Few tourists hire cars to see Egypt as it is usually less expensive and more comfortable to strike a bargain with a taxi driver or hire a chauffeur-driven car in the cities, and to travel between them by bus, shared taxi, train or air (see TRANSPORT).

Should you have special reasons for wanting a rental car, several local companies and one or two of the internationally known firms have offices in Cairo and representatives in other cities. Arrangements are: minimum age 25 years, with international driving licence or Egyptian driving licence, which can be obtained at the Giza station. Car rental must be paid in advance, either by credit card or cash (Egyptian pounds) or cash only (dollars).

CHILDREN. Many things to do in Egypt are fun for children. In Cairo, whisk to the top of the Cairo Tower for the panoramic view. On your way to the pyramids at Giza, detour to the Zoological Gardens just across the University (El-Gamaa) Bridge for a look at wildlife of Egypt and the Sudan. At the pyramids, older children will delight in a ride on a camel or horse, padding from one pyramid to the next.

In Luxor, horse-drawn carriages and Nile *feluccas* provide the means for adventure, while in Aswan these two are joined by other attractions: the botanical gardens on Kitchener's Island, the dramatic observatory-monument next to the High Dam, and the Philae Temples, which must be reached by boat.

Whether you plan to stay at a de luxe hotel with swimming pool or not, you can spend some time with the children at the poolside. Most hotels welcome visitors to use their pools for a small admission fee.

As to baby-sitters, your hotel room-boy or chambermaid will be glad to arrange for someone to stay with children; in luxury hotels the bell captain can provide someone. Rates vary, often depending on the bargain you strike with the sitter.

Can you get me a baby-sitter for tonight?   **múmkin tigíbli murabbía il-láyla**

CIGARETTES, CIGARS, TOBACCO★ *(sagáyir, sigár, tobákko).*
Familiar brands of internationally known cigarettes are readily available from kiosks and hotel news-stands. They cost about twice as much as Egyptian cigarettes, but are still quite reasonably priced by European standards. Cigars and pipe tobacco are found easily.

Shortages sometimes occur in the supply of Egyptian-made cigarettes. *Cleopatra* and *Nefertiti* are long filter brands, mild and flavourful; *Bustan* is a good quality unfiltered smoke; *Port Said* is the mentholated one.

A packet of…, please.	**élbit… min fádlak**
filter-tipped	**bifómm filtar**
without filter	**bidún filtar**
matches	**kabrít**

CLOTHING. Egypt's climate demands the coolest possible cotton clothing for a visit during the hot months from May to September, plus a broad-brimmed sunhat and sunglasses for both men and women. In Cairo and when visiting mosques, shorts (on either men or women) are out; women should have modest, longish dresses with sleeves, and a head-scarf, while men should wear trousers and a sports shirt.

A comfortable pair of sandals (as flat as possible) and a pair of flat walking shoes should cover footwear requirements for sightseeing and shopping any time of the year. Comfortable footwear is *essential* in Egypt for both the sand and rough stone terrain of the archaeological sites—as well as for the city centre where road-works are constantly in progress.

As most of Egypt's tourist hotels are luxury or first-class, men will feel more comfortable at dinner in a jacket-and-tie, though there is rarely a strict dress regulation.

In winter (November to March) it can be quite warm during the day but surprisingly chilly at night. A warm pullover or wrap and some light woollens are advisable.

Remember that Egyptian cotton is the best in the world, and shirts, gowns *(gallabiya)* and dresses are moderately priced—you needn't overload yourself with cottons from home.

COMMUNICATIONS. Postal service in Egypt is unpredictable. Postcards are taken less seriously than letters, and may be delayed. Even letters may take longer than anticipated. Allow plenty of time, or resort

C to telephone, telegraph or telex services for important messages. Also, have your mail sent care of your hotel rather than poste restante.

Post boxes can be bewildering: green boxes which bear a motorcycle picture are for express (special delivery) mail; blue, with an airplane, for air mail; red, with a train, for ordinary mail. In major cities, "express", "ordinary mail" and "air mail" are printed in block capitals in English on post boxes.

Hours: Cairo's main post office in Ataba Square is open from 8 a.m. to 3 p.m. and 5 p.m. to 7 p.m. daily except Friday. Other offices are open from 8.30 a.m. to 3 p.m. daily except Friday.

Telephone: Egypt's telephone system is undergoing extensive modernization, and service, especially in Cairo, has improved considerably. There have, however, been many changes to numbers in the process, so check them carefully.

Public telephones—which are rare but most commonly found in cigarette shops—may only be normal desk sets with a coin box attached. If you make a local call from your hotel room, you may be charged several times the normal rate. Almost all shops will allow you to use their telephone for local calls if you pay in advance.

To avoid hotel surcharges, go to a telephone office to place your call. You may have to wait some time before you get through, depending upon traffic—sometimes up to 24 hours.

Telegrams can be sent from telephone offices as well, and in Cairo, telex service is available too. Major hotels in Egypt have telex service at standard rates for guests, surcharged rates for outside users.

Dial 124 to send a telegram if you have a telephone and have paid a deposit.

Operator 140, 141 are for requesting telephone numbers, and 16, 180, 181 for telephone complaints, repairs, etc.

COMPLAINTS. In hotels, restaurants or shops, speak to the manager or proprietor; calm, courteous explanations of your complaint go a long way towards a solution, and a gentle hint that you are ready to appeal to a higher authority will usually break a deadlock. Most reputable establishments want to please you, so matters can usually be resolved quietly.

Should you have bigger problems, the tourism authorities are sympathetic, though the official complaint apparatus is ponderous. The quickest response comes from the Tourist Police, whose job it is to serve you and who take their duties seriously. See TOURIST INFORMATION OFFICES and POLICE for details.

CONVERTER CHARTS. For fluid and distance measures, see page 112. C
Egypt uses the metric system.

Temperature

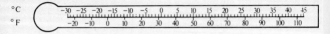

°C

°F

Length

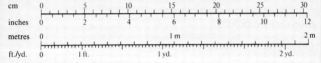

cm

inches

metres

ft./yd.

Weight

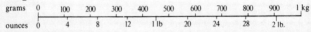

grams

ounces

COURTESIES. Egyptians long ago discovered the secret that a smile makes everything—and everyone—more pleasant. Though tipping may be a constant factor to reckon with in your dealings with many Egyptians, the smile is almost always sincere, and unrelated to the business in hand. Always shake hands upon meeting someone—Egyptians will often salute informally with the right hand before and after the shake. Other courtesies include never photographing someone without first asking his or her permission, and being very discreet about blowing your nose—especially in restaurants.

Egypt is one of the few Moslem countries in which non-Moslems are welcome to visit mosques. Be modestly dressed for your visit, remove your shoes before entering—an attendant will show you where to put them. It's better not to go to a mosque at prayer times, or on Friday, the Moslem holy day. If a few people are praying when you visit, avoid walking directly in front of them, and be careful not to disturb the tranquility of the place: as to taking pictures, use discretion.

Though tipping is found everywhere in Egypt (see BAKSHEESH) and it is usual to tip a guide or *gardien* of a mosque, tomb or ruin, from time to time a tip will not readily be accepted. Offer again; *some* Egyptians refuse several times just to show they don't require it from you.

111

C **CRIME and THEFT.** Though crime is low among Egyptians, petty theft and pickpocketing are as annoying as everywhere else. You should have no trouble if you take the normal precautions: watch your wallet or purse in crowded markets and on trains and buses, lock your luggage before giving it over to railway or airline porters, and don't leave valuables on open display in your hotel room. If you have been robbed, the Tourist Police (see POLICE) will do all they possibly can to recover your property.

D **DRIVING IN EGYPT**

To bring your car into Egypt you will need:
- International driving licence
- Car registration papers
- *Carnet de passage*

With the above documents, you may bring a car into Egypt without paying tax or having to pass an Egyptian driver's test. You will have to purchase third-party liability insurance in Egypt.

Driving conditions: Egyptian driving regulations were developed during the British tenure (though driving is on the right in Egypt), but many local customs have crept into usage; and the press of traffic and battling for parking spots makes it inadvisable for a tourist to drive in Cairo. Outside the capital, roads between the major towns are serviceable, but full of surprises such as slow-moving vehicles, broken roadbed, pedestrians and stray animals. For information on driving laws and help with any automobile matter, you can contact:

Automobile Club of Egypt, 10, Sharia Kasr el-Nil, Cairo.

Fluid measures

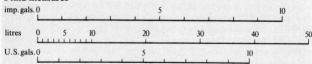

Distance

driving licence	**rókhsit alkiyáda**
insurance policy	**bolísit alta'mín**
Are we on the right road for…?	**húa da at-tarík li…**
Fill the tank, please.	**imlá il tank min fádlak**
normal/super	**ádi/súbar**
Check the oil/tires/battery, please.	**min fádlak shoof al zayt/al ágal/ al bataría**
I've had a breakdown.	**arabíyiti itattálit**
There's been an accident.	**fih hádsa**

D

ELECTRIC CURRENT. Most of Egypt has 220-volt, 50-cycle electric current. Exceptions are some parts of Heliopolis and Maadi (suburbs of Cairo), which have 110-volt current, although these areas are gradually changing to 220 volts. Sockets are the European type with two cylindrical prongs. Many hotels provide each room with a candle in case of power failure. Often, the current is not up to its full voltage strength.

E

What's the voltage, 110 or 220?	**kam al volt, míyya wa áshara (110) aww mitén wa ishrín (220)**

EMBASSIES and CONSULATES *(safára; konsolía)*

Australia: Embassy, Cairo Plaza, Corniche el-Nil, Boulac; tel. 777273/495/489.

Canada: Embassy, 6, Mohamed Fahmy el-Sayed Street, Garden City, Cairo; tel. 3543110.

Eire: Embassy, 3, Abul Feda Street, Zamalek; tel. 3408264, 3408547, 3414653.

United Kingdom: Embassy, 7, Ahmed Ragheb Street, Garden City, Cairo; tel. 3540850/2/9.
Consulate, 3, Mena Street, Roushdy, Alexandria; tel. 5467001/2.

U.S.A.: Embassy, 5, America el-Latineya Street, Garden City, Cairo; tel. 3557371.
Consulate, 110, Avenue El Horreya, Alexandria; tel. 4821911, 3572291, 3572391, 3572491.

EMERGENCIES. If your hotel receptionist or a Tourist Police officer is not at hand, you can telephone these numbers:

Police emergency	122
Ambulance	121
Fire Service	125

Any hospital has an ambulance service. Ambulance service can be slow because of the traffic.

ENTRY FORMALITIES and CUSTOMS CONTROLS. Everyone entering Egypt must register with the Interior Ministry at the "Mugamaa" in Tahrir Square, Cairo, within seven days of arrival. This may be done by the hotel, tour agent or host or individually. But it *must* be done. Late registration may entail a fine and a big bureaucratic row.

Visitors to Egypt need a valid passport and either a transit visa for a stay not exceeding seven days or a tourist visa for a period of one month (renewable for six months). Both are available from Egyptian consulates abroad, or from passport authorities at the point of entry for those who didn't manage to get them at home. The Egyptian visa system is now much better organized and one can be obtained at the airport upon entry quite rapidly. On leaving the country, visitors may change unused Egyptian money back into foreign currency provided they have kept *all* exchange receipts to prove they have spent at least L.E. 30 per day during their stay. However, this only applies to visitors travelling on their own, not to those on pre-paid tours arranged through an authorized travel agent.

The following items can be taken into Egypt duty-free and back into your own country:

Into:	Cigarettes		Cigars		Tobacco	Spirits		Wine
Egypt	200	or	25	or	200 g.	3 l.		
Australia	200	or	250 g. or		250 g.	1 l.	or	1 l.
Canada	200	and	50	and	900 g.	1.1 l.	and	1.1 l.
Eire	200	or	50	or	250 g.	1 l.	and	2 l.
N. Zealand	200	or	50	or	250 g.	1.1 l.	and	4.5 l.
U.K.	200	or	50	or	250 g.	1 l.	and	2 l.
U.S.A.	200	and	100	and	*	1 l.	or	1 l.

* a reasonable quantity

Visitors arriving from an infected country without an international vaccination against smallpox, cholera and yellow fever may be put into quarantine (check with your travel agent about current vaccination requirements which may vary).

Currency restrictions: You may not import or export more than L.E. 20 in local currency, but there is no restriction on the amount of foreign currency you may bring into or take out of Egypt as a foreigner, provided it is declared to customs on arrival. The law requires visitors to list *all* funds in their possession on an official currency declaration form. Demand the form if it is not offered and have it stamped at customs: it must be shown along with all currency exchange receipts when you leave the country. It is *very* important to have the currency declaration form available and in order, as customs officials may confiscate currency not entered on the form.

GUIDES* *(dalíl).* Only guides licensed by the Ministry of Tourism in Egypt are allowed into historical sites. You can arrange for a licensed guide through any hotel or travel agency, but it is good practice to specify in writing what you want and what you are willing to pay. Guides may or may not be very knowledgeable about antiquities, and may or may not be fully fluent in foreign languages.

We'd like an English-speaking guide.	**aízin dalíl bil lógha el-inglízi**
I need an English interpreter.	**aíz mutérgim inglízi**

HAIRDRESSERS' *(salón tagmíl).* It's wise to have an appointment if you plan to have your hair done on Thursday or Saturday, when barbers' and hairdressers' are busiest. Shops in Egypt have long hours, and the normal Monday closing is usually ignored by hotel shops.

Prices in the luxury hotels are like those at home—expensive by Egyptian standards, average by European.

HOTELS *(fóndok)* **and ACCOMMODATION*.** See also CAMPING, NILE CRUISES and YOUTH HOSTELS. Group tour operators usually have priority in room allotment, and so it is a good idea to go to Egypt with a group and to have the agent make all the arrangements. If you go on your own, make reservations far in advance, be sure they're confirmed, and then arrive in Egypt prepared to claim your room forcefully—reservations are sometimes ignored, no matter how iron-clad they may seem. The same goes for cruises on Nile boats—

H   make reservations early, and preferably in conjunction with a group tour. Competition for rooms is most intense during the prime months of the winter season, from December to April inclusive, except for Alexandria which is busiest in the hot summer months and virtually deserted from November to April.

Apart from, obviously, the fairly good and expanding selection of first-class hotels, the tremendous building spree of the last few years has resulted in the creation of a good range of medium-class hotels as well in Cairo.

Hotel rates are also quoted in US$ for foreigners. You can settle the bill by credit card or with Egyptian pounds—if the latter, you must have a receipt from the bank showing that you have changed hard currency.

HOURS. See also COMMUNICATIONS and MONEY MATTERS.

Shops

In Cairo, shops open from 10 a.m. to 7 p.m. in winter, from 10 a.m. to 8 p.m. in summer, closing one hour later on Mondays and Thursdays all year round. Governmental shops close between 2 and 5 p.m. every day. Although there is no consistency of closing for private shops, generally 2–5 p.m. is not a good time to shop throughout the year. Khan el-Khalili closes at 8 p.m. There are no fixed closing hours for shops during the month of Ramadan. A few close on Fridays, most on Sundays and some stay open until early morning.

Public services such as travel agencies, information offices, hairdressers and workshops are open during shop hours. Pharmacies stay open late.

Museums (in Cairo). Most are open every day of the week.

Largest and most important ones: 9 a.m. to 4 p.m., with a break from 11.30 a.m. to 1.30 p.m. on Fridays.

Smaller museums: 9 a.m. to 1 p.m., till 11.30 a.m. on Fridays.

These are the winter hours; in summer, some Cairo museums close at 2.30 p.m.

L   **LANGUAGE.** Arabic is not only the predominant and official language of Egypt, but Egyptian Arabic is widely regarded as a "standard" for the Arabic-speaking world in which dozens of Arabic dialects are found. Staff in large hotels usually speak some English and French, and perhaps a little German and Italian. If you need the help of a man on the street, English or French is the language to try.

The Berlitz phrase book ARABIC FOR TRAVELLERS covers most situations you're likely to encounter in your travels in Egypt.

Good morning	**sabáhil khayr**
Good evening	**masá'il khayr**
Good-bye	**ma'assaláma**
Thank you	**shúkran/muttshékkir**
Do you speak English?	**bititkállim inglízi**

LAUNDRY and DRY-CLEANING *(ghaséel; tandéef bil bokhár)*. Your hotel can arrange for laundry and dry-cleaning service, usually in its own plant. The best way to ensure quick service is to tip the chambermaid or room boy who takes the clothes, and stress the urgency of the situation. You may be surprised at the speed with which your clothes are expertly cleaned and returned.

When will it be ready?	**ímta takún gáhiza**
I need it…	**aízha…**
today/tomorrow	**ennahárda/bókra**

LOST PROPERTY. An appeal to the highest authority in a hotel or museum can help turn up lost or misplaced items. On the train, speak to the conductor, or the station-master when you alight. If you've left something in a taxi, the Tourist Police may be able to help, as records are kept of taxi movements between hotels, terminals and spots of touristic interest; for things left in "limousines" hired from Limousin Misr, contact the company (see TRANSPORT for details).

MEDICAL CARE. See also EMERGENCIES and ENTRY FORMALITIES. Ask your insurance company before leaving home if medical treatment in Egypt is covered by your policy. You might also want to have your doctor give you something against intestinal upset, just in case. Certain simple remedies can kill whatever-it-is quickly and effectively and maybe save a holiday from being spoiled.

Several specific medical risks exist on a trip to Egypt. In the hot months sunburn, sunstroke and dehydration are a constant danger, and preventative measures should be taken seriously. Bring insect repellant for use against flies and mosquitoes. Or buy one of the spray repellants readily available in Egypt, both local and imported; local brands tend to have more effect on local insect life. Less available is the rub-on repellant which is a useful item to pack, especially for sleeping with the

M window open. Also the waters of the Nile are inhabited by a dangerous parasite called bilharzia, contracted by ingesting unpurified Nile water, or through bare feet or skin in the water or along its banks. Don't swim in the Nile and don't walk barefoot near it.

Chemists'/Druggists' *(agzakhána).* Look for a sign with a blue crescent, and either a green cross or serpent within it, and you've found a shop that sells medicines. Many stay open long hours—even 24 hours a day. Though they may not have the exact medicine you want, they may have the same preparation made in Egypt and bearing a different (but usually similar) name. The Egyptian drug will be a great deal less expensive than the imported one. Here are some of Cairo's better pharmacies, that cater to both Egyptians' and visitors' needs:

Zarif, Talaat Harb Square; tel. 3936347.

Isaaf, 26 July Street; tel. 743369 (open day and night)

Pharmacie Dr. el Hakim, Osiris building, Latin America Street, Garden City; tel. 3540403.

I need a doctor/dentist.   **aíz doktór/doktór asnáan**

MEETING PEOPLE. See also ·COURTESIES. Egyptians have a long history of formal and flowery hospitality, now reduced to a few simple but very pleasant ceremonies. Tea, coffee, or a soft drink will be offered as soon as you take a seat in an office, shop or home. A friendly formality will prevail until you become better acquainted.

By the way, it is not customary for a host in a shop or office to give his guest his undivided attention; if there is an interruption, he will deal with it and then resume conversation with you. This method allows you to stay as long as you like without feeling you are keeping your host from his duties.

MONEY MATTERS

Currency: The Egyptian *pound* (L.E.) is divided into 100 *piastres* (pt.). You may see prices written several ways: L.E. 1.50, L.E. 1.500 or 150 pt.—which are all the same amount of money, one pound and a half.

Banknotes are found as 25 and 50 pt. and L.E. 1, 5, 10, 20 and 100.

Coins come in 5, 10 and 20 pts. Two different issues are in circulation

at present.

It's a good idea not to accept particularly ragged banknotes as you may have trouble getting others to accept them—except as tips. For currency restrictions, see ENTRY FORMALITIES AND CUSTOMS CONTROLS.

Banking hours: 8.30 a.m. to 2 p.m., Sunday to Thursday. All banks are closed on Fridays and Saturdays. Banking desks at the airports and in the lobbies of the larger hotels have special hours for the convenience of tourists.

Changing money: It is illegal to exchange foreign currency except at a bank or other authorized establishments, and it's also forbidden to pay for purchases in foreign currency. On board some Nile cruise boats, the purser is authorized to change money—be sure to obtain an official receipt. Always take your passport when changing money or traveller's cheques, and save the bank receipt which notes the transaction—you'll need it to reconvert Egyptian money to foreign currency. In fact, to avoid any conceivable problems or confusion, keep hold of all currency-exchange vouchers; you could be called upon to justify expenses, particularly hotel bills, plane tickets, etc., and to prove that you have not changed your money on the black market. Nothing worrying, just worth remembering.

At Cairo airport, there are bank desks before the check-in counters passport control.

In Alexandria there is a bank desk at the docks.

Credit Cards and Traveller's Cheques: More and more establishments accept credit cards. Traveller's cheques are readily cashed at banks.

NILE CRUISES*. Some hotels operate luxury-class cruise boats on the Nile, and many group travel firms charter less luxurious but still very comfortable boats and sell space on them through local travel agents. Your travel agent will be able to give you full particulars about accommodation on the boats, prices and departure dates. Rooms aboard cruise boats are often even more in demand than land-based hotel rooms in Egypt, so you'd do well to make arrangements as far in advance as possible. The normal itinerary is to fly to Luxor or Aswan (or go on the overnight train) and cruise between the two points for 5 to 8 days, stopping at major temples and ruins on the way. There are also trips

N from and to Cairo, usually at the beginning and end of the season. No matter how many days you stay on board, a Nile cruise will provide vivid memories for a life-time, and shouldn't be missed.

P **PHOTOGRAPHY.** Egypt has very few cloudy days, lots of bright sun, and sand and limestone which reflect a glaring light, so plan accordingly.

Virtually none of Egypt's important museums allows visitors to take photographs, and you will often be asked to leave your camera before entering a museum. By the same token, photography is forbidden inside the major tombs. Pictures may be taken (without flash) in most museums and tombs if a fee is paid for the camera.

Be careful not to take pictures of bridges, public buildings, airports, or any other subject which could be conceived as "military".

Always ask permission before taking photos of people or inside mosques—it's not appreciated if you simply photograph point blank.

May I take a picture?   **múmkin ákhod súra**

POLICE *(bolis)*. See also EMERGENCIES. Cairo and Alexandria city policemen wear white uniforms in summer, black in winter. In the provinces you'll see officers in khaki. Tourist Police officers, some of whom know a foreign language, have normal police uniforms, which have green and white armbands, with "Tourist Police" in English and Arabic written in red. You can contact the Tourist Police through any official Tourist Information Office.

In Cairo, the Tourist Police Public Service telephone number is 126. Their headquarters is at 5, Adly Street; tel. 2472584.

PUBLIC HOLIDAYS. Moslem religious holidays are also national holidays in Egypt. If a Moslem feast lasts more than a day, shops and offices will close on the first day, and open with shorter hours on the other days. During the Holy Month of Ramadan, when Moslems fast during daylight hours, shorter working hours apply almost everywhere in offices. Shops are open very late into the night. Coptic (Christian) holidays are not celebrated as national holidays, though Coptic-run shops and businesses may close. The Coptic calendar differs from the Gregorian one: Coptic Christmas, for instance, is always on January 7th.

Secular Holidays

January 1	New Year's Day (banks only)
first Monday after Coptic Easter	*Sham-en-Nessim* (National Spring Festival)
April 25	Sinai Day
May 1	Labour Day
June 18	Republic (Evacuation) Day
July 23	Revolution Day
October 6	Armed Forces (October Victories) Day
October 24	Suez Day
December 23	Victory Day

Religious Holidays. The Islamic *(Hegira)* calendar is lunar, with Moslem religious holidays falling 10 or 11 days earlier each year compared to the standard Gregorian calendar.

In Islamic reckoning, a day starts at sundown. If you're told tomorrow's a religious holiday, expect the celebrations to begin at sundown today. Businesses will close early on the eve of a holiday, and those restaurants which stay open may not serve alcoholic beverages.

RADIO and TV *(rádyo; tilivísyon).* Cairo has one television station broadcasting on three channels. Channel 2 has daily news bulletins in English and in French.

Egypt's multilingual radio station broadcasts from 7 a.m. to midnight daily, and in the course of the day has news and feature programmes in English, French, Italian, German, Greek and Armenian. For the schedule, consult the Cairo daily newspapers, *The Egyptian Gazette, Le Journal d'Egypte* or *Le Progrès Egyptien.*

RELIGIOUS SERVICES. Egypt is predominantly Moslem, with a sizeable Christian (mainly Copt) minority. Catholic and Protestant services are held in Cairo, Luxor and Aswan; in Cairo and Alexandria there are synagogues as well. For a complete listing of Sunday services, consult the Saturday issue of *The Egyptian Gazette,* called *The Egyptian Mail,* or the monthly magazine *Cairo Today.*

TIME DIFFERENCES. Egyptian time is one hour ahead of Central European Time, two hours ahead of G.M.T. during the winter. Clocks go forward one hour in summer.

T **TIPPING.** See also BAKSHEESH. Though a service charge is included in hotel and restaurant bills, you should leave an additional tip. You are also expected to give something extra to porters, bellboys, cinema and theatre ushers, etc., for their services. The chart below gives a few suggestions as to how much to leave.

Porter, per bag	L.E. 1
Maid, per week	L.E. 6
Waiter	10%
Table attendant	3–5%
Lavatory attendant	50 pt.
Taxi driver	50–100 pt.
Tour guide	10%
Hairdresser/Barber	10%
Felucca boatman	50 pt. per passenger

TOILETS *(twalét).* Public facilities are located in important museums and terminals, and you may use those in the larger hotels as well. If you use the facilities in a café or restaurant, it's usual to order a coffee or a bottled drink. The attendant will expect a small tip.

Toilets are usually marked with symbols of a man or a woman. Sometimes the attendant will direct you to use the "wrong" one, but he has his reasons—more often than not to do with failed plumbing—and will stand guard to prevent embarrassment.

Where are the toilets? **fayn al twalét**

TOURIST INFORMATION OFFICES. The Egyptian Ministry of Tourism has Tourist Information Offices in the larger Egyptian cities, and in many foreign countries as well. They can provide you with brochures, maps and other information on Egypt.

Cairo: Ministry of Tourism, 5, Adly Street; tel. 3903000 or 3901835. (Other offices at Cairo airport and at the Pyramids.)

Alexandria: Saad Zaghloul Square; tel. 4820258.

Luxor: Tourist Market, just south of Luxor Temple; tel. 82215.

Aswan: North of old part of town, just off Corniche; tel. 23297.

Egyptian Tourist Offices abroad:

Canada: Place Bonaventure 40, Frontenac, P.O. Box 304, Montreal, P.Q. H5A 1V4; tel. (514) 861-4420.

United Kingdom: 168 Piccadilly, London W. 1.; tel. (01) 493-5282.

U.S.A.: 630 Fifth Avenue, New York, N.Y. 10020; tel. (212) 246-6960.
323 Geary Street, Suite 608, San Francisco, CA 94102;
tel. (415) 781-7676.

TRANSPORT*. Transport in Cairo is overtaxed, to say the least. Buses are so crammed as to be impractical, and the intense traffic jams make even taxis less than speedy. For trips from the centre of Cairo to the Coptic sights of Old Cairo, you may try the Nile Bus which runs from the jetty opposite the Television Tower up river to the terminus at Old Cairo. A 5-minute walk takes you inland from the Nile bank to the Coptic quarter. The 40-minute journey makes about five stops en route and provides welcome relief from road traffic noise and congestion. The Metro stops at the Mar Girgis Station, which is in the Coptic area.

Taxis: Some taxis in Cairo and Alexandria have meters, but drivers cannot always be persuaded to run them—giving as an excuse that the machine is out of order. To avoid unpleasant surprises, fares should *absolutely* be agreed in advance. If a taxi driver does use the meter, the amount to expect is about twice the rate clocked up. You should know how to tell the driver your destination in Arabic as few know a foreign language (ask your hotel receptionist to write the address in Arabic). Taxi ranks exist near the larger hotels and tourist attractions (and at the airport), but the normal procedure is to stop a taxi in the street. Note that near each rank a Tourist Police officer will be on duty, laboriously recording the number of each cab, its time of departure and its destination.

   In towns where taxis have no meters, an official table of rates is established by the authorities, but it is sometimes difficult to discover what the correct fare should be. Often it is best to strike a bargain with the driver until you can get a list of fares from the Tourist Office.

Shared Taxis: Every city and town in Egypt has shared taxis for inter-city travel. Fares are fixed, cheap, and the cars move out once full. The majority are seven-seat Peugeots, the rest Mercedes. Fare-supervision is strict and very rarely will the driver ask for more. Tips are not expected. **123**

T Generally they will not operate, on a lengthy run, after 8 p.m. Cairo, of course, has several ranks—one for Alexandria, one for the canal cities, etc. The ranks are found close to the main railway station or bus station for a particular destination as the taxis absorb all the surplus traffic. Fares are very slightly more than the bus fare, sometimes less than the train fare (air-conditioned). Drivers will always approach you first. A group of four in a great hurry, for example, could leave immediately by buying the three remaining seats.

Chauffeur Service: Limousines provide a comfortable and reliable means of transport in Cairo. Be sure to agree on the fare beforehand.

Horse-cabs: The romantic horse-drawn carriages you'll see in Luxor and Aswan are governed by an official price list. Consult the list in the Tourist Office before you ride—you may have to haggle for a price in any case. There are even a few still in Cairo, if you can bear the traffic fumes!

Trains: Day trains operate frequently between Cairo and Alexandria from Cairo Station. Overnight trains equipped with sleeping and restaurant cars, and with air-conditioning, ply the route Cairo–Minia–Assiut–Luxor–Aswan and vice-versa. First class on the train is comfortable, second class is acceptable; make reservations early to avoid the disappointment of finding all seats and berths taken. There's also a special luxury tourist train between Cairo and Aswan, where meals and berths are included in the (relatively high) price.

Internal Air Routes: EgyptAir, sometimes called Misr Air in Egypt, operates modern and comfortable aircraft on flights between Cairo and Luxor and Aswan, with several flights a day depending on the season. There is also service to Abu Simbel from Cairo, Luxor and Aswan. You can visit the famous Temple of Ramesis for several hours, returning the same day; or you can reserve space on the next day's return flight and spend the night at one of the two hotels in Abu Simbel (have your reservations made in advance). There are also flights to the resort town of Hurghada.

ZAS Airline and Air Sinai also operate a domestic flight network.

Airport Transfers: Normal taxis and also Misr Travel cars and air-conditioned buses operate between Cairo airport and hotels in the city centre. The scramble for cars is sometimes intense, and it is not a bad idea to ask to share a cab with someone else—in Egypt, it's an accepted practice. Fares to various destinations are indicated on notice boards.

In Aswan and Luxor, both taxis and buses operate between the airports and central airline offices.

Taxi!	**taksi**
What's the fare to…?	**bekám li …**
Take me to…	**khódni li …**

WATER *(máyya)*. Egyptians have a saying that if a visitor drinks even a little water from the Nile, he will return to Egypt for sure. Tap water in Aswan, Luxor and Cairo comes from the Nile by way of a purification plant, and is safe to drink though not very tasty. Whatever you do, don't drink *directly* from the Nile.

The local brand of mineral water is called Helwan. Another one, jointly produced with Vittel of France, is called *Baraka*. It is perfectly acceptable to take the unfinished portion of a litre of mineral water along with you from a restaurant or hotel dining room.

I'd like some mineral water.	**aíz máyya ma'daníyya**
fizzy (carbonated)/still	**gazzíyya/áada**
Is this drinking water?	**di máyya lil shurb**

YOUTH HOSTELS *(bayt shabáb)*. Hostels in Egypt's main cities offer students and hostellers a place to stay for a very low price, though standards of comfort vary. The best hostels are often full, and so advance reservations by mail are advised. For full information contact:

The Egyptian Youth Hostel Association, 7, Doctor Abdel Hamid Said Street, Marrouf, Cairo; tel. 758099.

There are hostels located at:

Cairo:	Al Manyal Youth Hostel, 135, Abdel Aziz al-Saud Street, Manyal; tel. 840729.
Alexandria:	El-Shatbi New Youth Hotel, 23, Port Said Street, Shatbi; tel. 75459
Luxor:	Corniche Street
Aswan:	Abtal El-Tahrir; tel. 2313.

Index

An asterisk (*) next to a page number indicates a map reference.